THE CLUE
TO
CHRISTIAN EDUCATION

The

Clue to Christian

Education

BY

Randolph Crump Miller

NEW YORK
CHARLES SCRIBNER'S SONS

Dedicated to

The Mother of My Four Girls

MURIEL HALLETT MILLER

1913–1948

PREFACE

FOR the past several years I have been concerned about the apparent failure of Christian educators to take seriously into account the problem of the relation of the content of the Christian revelation to the best creative methods of teaching. The difficulty was not too hard to define, and several books and articles outlined the weaknesses in Christian educational philosophy, with H. Shelton Smith's *Faith and Nurture* being the chief stimulus to my thought, but no one pointed to a solution. The "clue" had not been discovered.

A summary of the problem appeared in *Christianity and the Contemporary Scene*,[1] in which it was said that "life-centered teaching is sound psychologically, pedagogically, and philosophically. It is the natural and quickest way to learn. There were, however, two errors which were frequently made by the educators. First, the method became an end in itself, and thus the direction of action and belief was veiled or lost. Second, what was taught was the product of a dated liberal doctrine, and therefore soon was not consistent with what the majority of the people wanted taught."

I stated the needs as follows: "A theology for Christian education is needed. The objectives, theory, and methods of Chris-

---

[1] Edited by Henry H. Shires and Randolph C. Miller. New York: Morehouse-Gorham, 1943, pp. 196–201.

tian education need to be undergirded and perhaps altered by
a more self-conscious theological reconstruction. . . . At the
same time, there needs to be a facing of the problem of relating content to method in an organic whole."

There were other problems which bothered me at the time,
especially the need for evangelism as part of the educational
program and the need for parent participation.

I found as I thought upon the problem that the "clue"
would be found in the relevance of theology to the whole of
life, and that with this clue I could open the doors of the
associated questions of method, evangelism, and parent cooperation.

The opening chapter is a brief description of what I believe
the clue to be. The remainder of the book is an elaboration of
theory in terms of the relevance of specific theological beliefs
to the lives of adults and children of various ages. I have not
been concerned primarily with method except as it illustrates
the theory.

*   *   *   *

The title of the book came from my first wife, shortly before her death. She asked me what I was driving at, and I
said, "I think I have the clue to the whole problem," and she
answered, "There's your title, 'The Clue to Christian Education.' "

Many friends have offered help and encouragement, especially fellow members of the Editorial Board of the Department of Christian Education of the Protestant Episcopal
Church: Dr. V. O. Ward, Mrs. Dora Chaplin, Dr. John
Heuss, Dr. Reuel L. Howe, and Canon Gardner Monks. Mrs.
Nelle Wagar Darby, Mrs. Mildred Scheel, and Miss Anne
Shields in Berkeley have assisted in various ways, and my
mother-in-law, Mrs. P. Shaul Hallett, has read my manuscript
and watched my children. New insights and blessings have

come to me as Elizabeth Fowlkes Miller and I have built a new family life around her two children and my four.

The following abbreviations have been used to identify the translations of the Bible: A—*The Revised Standard Version of the New Testament* (copyright 1946 by the International Council of Religious Education), G—*The Bible: An American Translation*, translated by J. M. Powis Smith and Edgar J. Goodspeed (University of Chicago Press), M—*The Bible, a New Translation*, by James Moffatt (Harpers), B—*The New Testament in Basic English* (Dutton), P—*Letters to Young Churches: A Translation of the New Testament Epistles*, by J. B. Phillips (Macmillan), PB—*Book of Common Prayer*, KJ—*The Holy Bible*, King James version. I am indebted to the publishers of these versions of the Bible in those instances where they have given me permission to quote from a particular translation.

RANDOLPH CRUMP MILLER

Church Divinity School of the Pacific
Berkeley 9, California

CONTENTS

CHAPTER ONE
THE CLUE

THERE is something new in the theory and practice of Christian education. It is coming out of parents' and teachers' meetings in terms which they do not often understand; it is being expressed by pastors in their dissatisfaction with both the older methods of teaching and the newer and progressive methods; it is being illustrated by the demand for new lesson materials, by the experiments being made among the educational leaders of the various denominations, and by the increasing cooperation between home and Church.

It is hard to put one's finger on the exact problem, because the difficulty now confronting us is being expressed primarily in negative terms. There is increasing dissatisfaction with the content-centered teaching which is still prevalent, and there is also widespread distrust of the so-called life-centered teaching. This vagueness of analysis is further illustrated by the enthusiasm with which new tricks have been tried: There are no answers to the basic problem in novel teaching methods, in the use of motion pictures and other visual aids, or in expanded time for the education of both children and adults, important as these things are.

Some of the difficulties of the older materials were overcome by turning to the experience of the learner as a basic element in educational procedure. The earlier methods had been catechetical, or ungraded, or Bible centered, with no thought for the religious needs and experiences of the pupils. To get away from this emphasis on content, it was decided to begin at the "growing edge" of the learner and lead him through his increased interests and insights toward a fuller and richer Christian life. Too often, the procedure was reversed, so that "a little child shall lead them" not to the deepest truths of Christian living, but to the vagaries of childhood or the mutual interchange of ignorance of high school students in a bull session or the prejudices of ill-informed adults. As a matter of fact, the main goal of education was lost sight of just as much in life-centered as in content-centered teaching, for the goal of all education is quite clearly to learn "truth," and there is no easy way to acquire or impart "truth."

This points to the fundamental weakness in practically all educational theory: *a failure to grasp the purpose of Christian education and to impart Christian truth.* "Ye shall know the truth, and the truth shall make you free," we are told; but when the emphasis has been on truth, there has been no method adequate to impart it; and when there have been effective methods, there has been no fundamental truth to guide them. Our philosophy of educational method has been sound at the expense of theology, while both true and false theologies have been presented without the methods to bring them to life in the experiences of the learners.

Let us illustrate this thesis: It is true that a little child learns primarily through activity, and that what he sees or touches or smells is of greater significance than what he hears. He can learn great lessons about God because he can see, touch, or smell a flower or a doll or a baby. But too often he achieves romantic and unrealistic views of natural processes because the interpretation is not fundamentally either scientific or Christian, and as a result he will have to unlearn this meaning of nature as he grows older.

A child in the fifth grade may spend a great deal of time making a relief map of Palestine. This is an enjoyable occupation, and he will be able to show the routes which Jesus followed from Nazareth to Jerusalem, and he will understand the deadness of the Dead Sea and the sudden storms on the Lake of Galilee. Too often such knowledge will bring him no closer to seeing what it means to accept Jesus as the Christ, and while his geographical insights may have improved greatly and he may have become a quite adequate map maker, he will be no farther along the road to becoming a Christian. This type of worthwhile and exciting activity will keep him occupied, and the methodology is fundamentally sound, but unless "something new has been added," it will result in an actual stoppage of Christian growth.

The examples on the other side are equally frustrating. There was a time when the same Bible story was taught to each age-group and all learners were treated alike, because, if the story were in the Bible it had to be taught some day. While it is generally admitted that this is impossible today even in the smallest ungraded Church school, there are still many hangovers in educational circles. First grade children are expected to recite and understand the Apostles' creed. Uniform lessons are still among the best sellers of Church school materials. The catechism is still taught in terms of set questions and answers. Some parents and Church school leaders are disturbed when their children do not learn by rote Bible verses which are so many meaningless jumbles to the youngsters, although it is recognized that the right use of memorization is valuable.

The dissatisfaction with the dilemmas has led the writers of Church school courses to seek a new solution. They have not worked out a theory, but there is in their efforts a hint to the proper theory. The newest Bible courses have not been placed simply on a problem-solving level. It has been discovered that the Bible is not only the source of potential solution to many problems, but that it has within it the power to suggest new questions to which it has the answer. So it has been that courses have been worked out which make full use of the specific problems of a particular age-group, but which lead them also into the mystery of the Bible as something worth knowing in itself. The same thing has been done with Church history, so that whereas historical processes and events are understood in terms of modern problems, they are also comprehended within the framework of the situations actually facing the historical actors and writers. Clues to a solution of the problem have also been provided by the writers of courses on worship, for it has been discovered that worship is the experience-centered method *par excellence* for educational purposes, that worship is an activity of one who knows himself to be in the presence of God, to whom the worshiper brings his own difficulties and in the presence of whom he finds solace and power and blessing. Courses on Christian ethics have also stumbled on this same truth, that the central beliefs of the Christian tradition are relevant to present-day living.

I

But the insights of such discoveries, important as they are, do not quite get at the heart of the problem. *The major task of Christian education today is to discover and impart the relevance of Christian truth.* The one missing topic in most educational schemes today is *theology*, and in theology properly interpreted lies the answer to most of the pressing educational problems of the day. The new element in educational theory is the discovery of the organic relation between doctrine and experience, between content and method, between truth and life.

Now before this is misunderstood, two things must be said. This is not a plea to return to a content-centered curriculum, for it is perfectly clear that an emphasis on content as an end in itself leads to verbalism, whereby the learner repeats the words but is not concerned with the meaning. That is like trying to Christianize a parrot, and success cannot be achieved by that method. In the second place, it is not a desire to return to indoctrination, for indoctrination implies a kind of authority which is consistent with controlled propaganda rather than with the growth of individuals in the Christian way of life.

But if neither content nor indoctrination provides the clue, how can theology be at the center of the curriculum? The answer is that theology is *not* at the center. *The center of the curriculum is a twofold relationship between God and the learner. The curriculum is both God-centered and experience-centered. Theology must be prior to the curriculum!* Theology is "truth-about-God-in-relation-to-man." In order to place God and man at the center of the Christian educational method, we must have adequate knowledge of the nature and working of both God and man, and of God's relationships to particular pupils.

For example, it would be possible to work out a sound curriculum based on the Apostles' creed (assuming that the creed is true in so far as it may be proved by Scripture and made meaningful in experience). But the creed would be placed *back of* the curriculum rather than in it. It would be introduced into the curriculum in terms of the relevance of Christian truth to the experiences and capacities of the learners, until at the proper level it could be studied as a summary of truths which are relevant to Christian living today. Most of us would not think of this as an adequate curriculum, unless it were enriched by the many implications of the creed (and if the space of time indicated by the punctuation between "Mary, suffered" were taken seriously, we could teach the life of

Christ), but there would be a depth of meaning and a richness of experience provided by even so inadequate a curriculum which are lacking in most modern approaches to Christian education.

The task of Christian education is not to teach theology, but to use theology as the basic tool for bringing learners into the right relationship with God in the fellowship of the Church. We have tried the Bible as a tool, and have ended up with some knowledge of the Bible but with no basic principles for using it properly. It is true that Holy Scripture is the basic authority for theology, but it is also evident that theology is a guide to the meaning of the Bible. Theology provides the perspective for all subjects, and yet all subjects are to be taught in terms of the interests and capacities of the learners in their relationship to God and to their fellow men.

When we say that truth is the underlying principle of the curriculum, this does not mean that we can be dogmatic about it. We need to recognize the great varieties of concepts held to be true by various individuals and denominations calling themselves Christian, and then to grant that our teachers will be bound to a theological system in terms of their own loyalty and freedom. The degrees of authority and freedom will vary from communion to communion, and from congregation to congregation within a communion, so that the writer of lesson materials and the teacher of a class will still have to use their own intelligence in making selections of theological tools for religious instruction.

There is great danger in this approach, as we have said, for it opens the door to the emphasis on content at the expense of Christian growth, and it could bring us back to the old idea of indoctrination, but the safeguard against this error is the insistence that there is a proper *relationship* between content and method. It is this relationship which needs further investigation. If we are right in our assumption that theology lies back of the curriculum and is to be introduced into it in the light of the "growing edge" of the learner, we need to understand the relation of theology to Christian living at the various age-levels, and this involves what is even more fundamental: the relevance of theology for all of life.

A person's behavior is guided by his deepest convictions, for what he believes in his inmost self determines his actions. His motivations are organically related to this theology. He may hold these concepts consciously or unconsciously. He may behave in a way foreign to a creed which he deceives himself into thinking he accepts, and thus may indicate that his basic drives are other than what he professes (and the hypocrite is one who professes one set of beliefs and acts according to another set). The complexity of his personality and the confusion of his motives may blur the picture of the relation between his beliefs and his behavior. But when the principle of this relationship is applied consistently and with due regard for all the factors, it will be discovered that the beliefs which are *habitually* held (and thus taken seriously even when one is not conscious of them) are the normal bases for action.

If this be true, it is of the greatest significance for Christian education. It explodes both the traditional view and the progressive one, for the traditional view insists that beliefs be accepted within the framework of a certain vocabulary regardless of their relevance, while the progressive view ultimately is reduced to the solving of a problem within the frame of reference of that problem and without regard to the wider cosmic or metaphysical point of view. If theology comes into the foreground of Christian teaching, there is great danger that beliefs will be held which are not part of one's basic personality pattern, whereas if theology is disregarded there is no sense of ultimate purpose. ⸿

Theology in the background; faith and grace in the foreground might well be the slogan for this new point of view.

The center of the educational process is neither theology nor the individual learner. *The purpose of Christian education is to place God at the center and to bring the individual into the right relationship with God and his fellows within the perspective of the fundamental Christian truths about all of life*—a Christian view of the universe, a Christian view of God who is known in experience and in the historical process, a knowledge of Jesus Christ who is to be accepted as Lord and Savior, a view of man which actually accounts for the experiences of damnation and salvation, an acceptance of the Church as a people-church in a covenant relationship with God, and the experience of the learner in terms of the *realities* underlying these concepts. When such a relationship between content and method is achieved, theology becomes relevant to Christian living, and education is almost synonymous with evangelism. Evangelism has often been ignored or misunderstood in modern educational circles, but its essential purpose can never be ignored if Christian education is to remain a vital force in the life of the Church. To evangelize is to confront men with Jesus Christ, so that they will put their trust in God through him, and by the power of the Holy Spirit live as Christ's disciples in the fellowship of the Church.

The person who by faith comes to this position is said to be integrated. The integration of the personality which is the goal of religious instruction can never be achieved in terms of ideals alone (as in character education), or of beliefs alone (as in indoctrination), or of social adjustment alone (as in much modern psychiatry). Just at the point where Christianity is unique, its educational philosophy and its methods have fallen down. The weakness of the good man who lacks religion is that his personality is centered on ideals and he becomes like the Pharisee in Jesus' parables. The charge against religious fanatics is that they know Bible verses and creeds, but have little insight into the meaning of Christlikeness. The trouble with many who have made good social adjustments is that they lack the divine discontent which is the only motivation for making a better world.

There must be a deeper integration. Theology, in so far as it represents truth, points in the direction of a Christian answer, which is that Christian integration lies in the relationship between God and man. It is the integration which results from a deep and abiding personal relationship between God and man. It flows from a right religious adjustment which is a basic process of living. It is more than intellectual or emotional or volitional activity, for it involves the total personality in relation to the ultimate reality, who is God. The human integration of a child does not evolve from his *idea* of his parents. It comes from his *relationship* with his parents. So also, his religious integration does not come primarily from his *idea of God*. It comes from his *personal relationship* with God.

It is central to the educational theory of these chapters to recognize the radical nature of Christian integration. Modern studies in psychology point toward the same emphasis: a man's integration is in terms of the organic relation between himself and his environment, not in terms of ideas or values but in terms of the situation in which he finds himself. It is Christian theology which adds a further element, that central in the Christian's environment is the living God and that the frame of reference for Christian living is he in whom we live and move and have our being. The Epistle to the Ephesians describes it as "reaching maturity, reaching the full measure of development which belongs to the fulness of Christ—instead of remaining immature, blown from our course and swayed by every passing wind of doctrine, by the adroitness of men who are dexterous in devising error; we are to hold by the truth, and by our love to grow up wholly unto Him" (Eph. 4:13–15, M).

No current educational theory adequately accounts for this end-product of a sound program of Christian education. That children have grown up in the Church and come to a religion of maturity is an acknowledged fact, but it has never been the conscious aim of the educational system within the Churches as far as statements of purpose and method are concerned. Horace Bushnell's *Christian Nurture,* with its concern for the relationship between home and Church as the matrix of Christian nurture, came the closest to seeing this point of view, but those who used Bushnell's insights never adequately comprehended the organic connection between content and method, and they blurred the necessary relation between home and Church. Out of the tremendous concern for the present situation in Christian educational circles, Paul Vieth's *The Church and Christian Education* deals with all the factors involved, and Ernest Ligon's *A Greater Generation* is an important contribution to understanding the role of parents in the Church's program, but it has not been made clear how we can use the most effective of modern educational methods to teach a profoundly Christian theology in terms of the relationship between deeply held convictions and Christian behavior.

Those who are aware of the theological deficiencies in modern education have failed to see clearly the answer to the problem. The solution is not to inject theology into an otherwise non-theological approach to Christian education, for that is to get caught in the vicious circle of repeating the cycle of old mistakes. Theology, which is truth from a Christian perspective, must be the presupposition of any curriculum. There is a proper theological perspective for using the Bible, for examining the life of Christ, for approaching Christian history, for studying the meaning of worship and of the sacraments, for finding the Christian answer to individual behavior problems, for looking on the social situation, and for building Christian fellowship between the Churches.

For the Churches corporately to find an answer to such problems as these, means that the educators must become theologians, and the theologians must become educators, and the writers of lesson materials must be grounded thoroughly in both educational theory and theological method. Every aid must be sought from the findings of child and adult psychology, secular educational experience, and the sociology of learning, and in so far as the underlying theological presuppositions are sound, the Church's educational system may make use of the findings of all the sciences related to secular educational theory.

II

Other elements enter the picture as we examine the clue to Christian education. There are the practical problems of insufficient funds, inadequate time during the week for Christian education, untrained teachers in the Church schools, untrained and sometimes indifferent clergy, and improper equipment. These are difficult barriers to overcome even when the theory is sound, although it is not our purpose to deal with them in these chapters.

There are other elements in the theory of education which must be brought to bear on the present situation. The first of these is an understanding of the place of the home in the educational development of little Christians. It is a generally acknowledged fact that the little child gets his fundamental training in religious and character development before he is exposed to any kind of formal education in school or Church. The patterns of his reactions to all kinds of stimuli are built into habits during the early years. There is little chance that the Church in one hour or so per week (and against the background of a secular home and school) can do more than build on the habit patterns already established. Therefore, it is important that the significance of the relation between home and Church be realized within the elementary educational theory of the Church. The Christian home may be the greatest aid to the Church, and through their mutual interdependence there is the opportunity for a more sound and permanent Christian education.

Experiments along these lines are being carried out in many areas of the Church's life. There are experiments in the pre-school age-group, where parents are assisted by the Church in providing the conditions under which Christian growth may be furthered. So far, the Church has not been prepared to provide adequate guidance to parents, but the realizing of the need for this type of cooperation merits our hope that something significant may develop in terms of a new educational philosophy.

Cooperation between parents and the Church is really just beginning at the point where the child enters Church school, but often that is where they are cut off. Yet if there is to be any significant relationship between what is done at Church school and the child's daily life, the cooperation of parents is equally necessary at this point, and throughout the adolescent period as well. Some new lesson materials make a place for the parents in their methods, and in more advanced plans parents must actually take part in the Sunday schedule and then be ready to make reports on the progress of their children. While parents at the beginning of such an experiment are unprepared to give much help, by proper education they may become more effective than the average teacher. At this point, the educational theory is sound but it needs to be implemented as it is put into more widespread practice.

Because religion deals so much with intangibles, with subtly changing attitudes, and with the development and growth of the spirit, it is often hard to measure progress. Parents have been enlisted to assist in measuring the improved spiritual characteristics of their children, and teachers have been instructed in recognizing the changes which indicate successful teaching. In the past, too often the only measure of a child's religious growth has been in his ability to memorize or recite various selections of words, which as an end in itself might be a worthwhile exercise in memory but which has practically no effect on the child's relation to God. In reaction against content-centered teaching, we have quite rightly discarded the emphasis on memory work as a token in itself of Christian development, but we still have not discovered how to make the truths of the Christian Gospel relevant to everyday living in terms which can be observed. The intangibles have remained too intangible to be seen, and yet only as Christians learn to practice and bear witness to the Gospel can there be any significant growth in wisdom and in favor with God and man. Our clue to Christian education does not point to an easy answer to this question, but it poses the problem in different terms, in that it insists that *Christian growth is a process of increased integration centered on the living God who is in our midst.*

In modern society, the home usually finds that the basic implications of daily living are based upon a secular philosophy. The family exists in a society which is governed by the mechanics of industrialism and by the economics of the profit system, and it is against this cultural infiltration that the Christian home must work. It is not a problem of building a Christian home in a Christian society (and indeed the problem has never been that simple); it is rather the discovery of the relevance of the Christian home within a society which permits, condones, and approves many un-Christian motives and actions.

Our fundamental educational procedures in the public schools are based primarily upon the principles of a secular society. While it is true that Christianity provides the religious nucleus of American culture, it is also evident that the predominant educational philosophy of the United States is a pragmatic and instrumentalist approach which has little or no place for religion. The public schools, important and significant as they are in American culture, are hardly allies of the Christian Church and Christian home in the field of basic theological motives and assumptions. The school may well be an ally in terms of cooperative activities, and it may supplement the work of the Church and home without distorting what the Christian is trying to achieve, but there is an underlying difference of philosophy which must be recognized.

The child is exposed first of all to the influence of his parents, and this is where the crucial influence on character development takes place. At a certain point, the schools begin to have as much as or more influence than the parents, although the parents never cease to have an obligation in this regard. The Church is always on the sidelines, making use of whatever experiences the home and school and community provide for a Christian interpretation of life. This means that the Church should often sit in judgment on the child's experiences which run in opposition to the basic assumptions of a Christian society. At other times, the Church will find in these experiences rich and abiding meanings which are ways of opening the child's awareness of God.

The Church also provides a new set of experiences, which are the product of the Church's life of worship, study, fellowship, and service. These are small elements in the time span of the child, totaling at most only a little over an hour or two per week, but their significance far outweighs the brevity of the experiences. If conditions in the home and school are sufficiently related to what happens in Church, the Church becomes relevant as a basis for providing the deeper and richer meanings of life. But in many instances, the Church provides an isolated kind of experience, where the child fails to see the relevance of what is happening, and thus he sees religion as divorced from life. This is due not only to a false concept of the Church's relation to society or to the inadequacy of educational method. The real failure is due to the inability to relate theology to life, and thus we are back to our original analysis that the weak link in modern Christian education is the failure to realize the proper place of the relevant truths of Christianity *behind* the child-centered and God-centered experiences of the learners. When theology is meaningful and related to life, it is possible to make use of the experiences of all of life to build a Christian perspective in the light of the learner's situation and age-group, illuminating those experiences with the peculiarly Christian experiences of worship, sacrament, preaching, study, fellowship, and work as found within the life of the Church.

III

The clue to Christian education is the rediscovery of a relevant theology which will bridge the gap between content and method, providing the background and perspective of Christian truth by which the best methods and content will be used as tools to bring the learners into the right relationship with the living God who is revealed to us in Jesus Christ, using the guidance of parents and the fellowship of life in the Church as the environment in which Christian nurture will take place.

I believe the clue rests in the picture of Jesus as a teacher or rabbi in the Gospels. He always assumed the basic truth of belief in God. He taught that God was our Father. He referred constantly to the fundamental truths revealed in the Old Testament. His theology was relevant to every situation in which he found himself. But he always taught in terms of a particular problem or of a specific individual or group. He related his theology to life. He spoke to the "growing edge" of his hearers, and he always led them beyond himself to a deeper loyalty to the Father. His parables were always "life situations" to his hearers, and they saw the application of his teaching to their problems. He never watered down his theology, but he always made it speak to the situation. He did not speak or teach in abstractions.

So also, we are dealing with real children and real adults, and theology is simply "truth-about-God-in-relation-to-man." As adults, we should have mature beliefs, but we should teach these beliefs in terms of the experiences and capacities of the children and older learners, leading them always from their "growing edge" to the deeper meanings and appreciations of life. The chief source of all our teaching is the Bible, the chief interest of our teaching is the learner, and the chief end of our teaching is the God and Father of Jesus Christ.

Because Christianity is primarily an historical rather than a metaphysical religion, the center of the approach to God will be through Jesus Christ, and Jesus will always be seen against the historical background of the Incarnation. While one would not tell a kindergarten child that the Christmas story tells of the birth of the "incarnate Lord" and expect him to understand the phraseology, it would be necessary for the teacher and the writer of the lesson material to know this and to teach so that the child would not learn something foreign to this belief. Some educators might even decide that it would be better not to emphasize the "baby Jesus" at the expense of later Christian faith, for sometimes a child fails to get beyond thinking of Jesus as a baby. In other words, method and content would be judged both by mature theological considerations and by sound knowledge of how the child's personality reacts.

We have acquired a great deal of information concerning the behavior and thoughts of the little child, we have experimented widely and wisely with the learning process at all age-levels, and we have made great use of these new insights, but we have never brought theology to bear upon them. Theology has been taught in opposition to child psychology, and this has been done at the expense of both theology and the child. The new task is to make theology relevant, realizing that the goal of Christian education is Christian truth, that truth may be acquired only through the interpretation of experience, and that we become Christians only as we use truth to place ourselves in commitment to the living God revealed to us in Jesus Christ and through the fellowship of the Church.

To make this specific, it is our intention in the succeeding chapters to take the basic theological presuppositions of a Christian educational philosophy, and to illustrate how the clue described in this chapter may be used in actual situations to realize the objectives of a theologically sound Christian education.

CHAPTER TWO

THE FOCAL POINT

THE center of the entire system of any educational process which can rightly be called "Christian" is Jesus Christ. The oldest question asked of a mature and confessing Christian is: "Do ye promise to follow Jesus Christ as your Lord and Savior?" This is the focal point of Christian faith, and it follows that it is also the basic theological assumption behind any educational philosophy which is adequate for Christian purposes. If parents and teachers are to give their children an abiding faith in Christ, they must understand their own relationship to the Lord of life and death.

The whole of the Christian religion lies ultimately in a personal relationship between the believer and the God of Jesus Christ. It is loyalty to Christ which in turn leads to the integration of the disciple arising from this relationship. The mature Christian, living in the congregation of the faithful, finds his wholeness in the worshiping community which is called "the Body of Christ."

If we take this central affirmation of Christian faith seriously, it will serve to illustrate the underlying thesis of these chapters, which is that we need to place theology in the background as the basic perspective and framework for all educational procedures. The degree to which a theology is consistent with experience and relevant to daily living determines the standard of educational effectiveness in its leading of children and adults into the Christian way.

It is our view that this may be accomplished with any theology in so far as that theology is true and relevant. Some success could be achieved against the background of Protestant Fundamentalism, Greek Orthodoxy, Roman Catholicism, or ethical culture with Christian overtones. Therefore, the reader does not have to subscribe to the theological tenets of this writer in order to gain insight into this educational philosophy. However, it is the contention of these chapters that the beliefs presented are both true and relevant, and therefore must be taken seriously as a sound background for Christian teaching in the twentieth century. These beliefs need to be stated on an adult level, in terms of mature experience, and then comes the problem of translating each belief in terms of the experiences and limitations of the learners of a particular age-group, and in turn making such a belief relevant to their daily living.

I

The proper starting point of Christian education is to face up to the challenge of the meaning of Christ, to discover what faith in Jesus Christ as Lord and Savior actually implies in terms of today's problems of living, and to be sure of the truth of the conclusions reached. To avoid this central question of Christian faith, as some writers of lesson materials and teachers, parents, and pastors have done, means enfeebling the educational system of the Church at its very heart.

There are serious problems to be solved on theological grounds long before we begin worrying about the proper age for introducing the life of Christ; we need to know what the Cross means prior to reaching a conclusion concerning the adolescent attitude toward the crucifixion; we need to have a concrete idea of the relevance of the Atonement and Incarnation to our own lives before we can start to apply it to the lives of children.

The educators are aware of this problem. There is a great deal of good and sound theology in Paul Vieth's *The Church and Christian Education,* and this volume reflects the considerations of a committee of the International Council of Religious Education. Dr. Vieth writes, "The focus of Christian revelation is found in Jesus Christ. He is the embodiment of the Gospel, the good news of the saving grace and power of God. In him God was reconciling the world to himself. God commended his love toward us in the death of his Son. Here was more than man's utmost devotion to the divine will. Here was the redemptive act of God himself through a human life in history." [1]

Not only is the problem of the nature of Christ the focal point in Christian education, it is also the major question in theological circles. This is nothing new, for the size of the paragraphs in the Apostles' and Nicene creeds reminds us that the earliest Christian controversies were on this same subject. There is an unresolvable conflict at the heart of any discussion of the nature of Christ; the theologian either must face up to a dilemma or select one horn; and this paradoxical issue has never been settled to anyone's satisfaction throughout the history of the Church. There is never more than an uneasy alliance within the person of Christ in any theory about his nature. This kind of dialectic is difficult enough for adults to follow, and it is almost impossible to translate into the concepts or the experiences of children.

Lack of awareness of the problem leads to a watered-down Christology on the one hand or a non-human Jesus on the other. Both solutions have appeared in many theologies and in many sets of Church school materials. But a satisfactory

[1] *The Church and Christian Education,* St. Louis: Bethany Press, pp. 66–67.

statement of Christology should be possible and should be
relevant to daily living.

This dualism in Christology stems directly from the problem itself. There are those who begin with the conviction that
Jesus is personally the incarnation of God, sharing God's
nature, and therefore different in kind from any other creature.
This leads quite naturally to the difficulty of understanding
how God could submit to being finite, of how Jesus could have
been in error on any subject, and of how he could have prayed
as a man to his Father. The earliest heresies of the Church had
their origin in this starting point, for it was difficult to hold
the deity of Jesus and then to move to a position recognizing
his limitations in being a man.

There are others who begin with the historic record of the
life of Jesus, and in him they find the highest revelation of
God ever received by or through men; they see in him the
characteristics of deity, but the moral grandeur of the man
Jesus stands out so clearly in his life and death and resurrection that they are not upset when it is clearly stated that he
did not know all things. Here also there is difficulty, the opposite difficulty of those in the first group, for the problem is to
explain how *a man* can at the same time be the second Person
of the Trinity, mediating a final revelation of the true God.
This argument leads, if pressed too far, to the Unitarian
position.[2]

Either of these positions, held alone, leads not only to heresy
but to absurdity. They are simply bad theology because they
are untrue to the facts of Christian experience. We cannot
say, with one writer, that "the historical Jesus is a corpse,"
because he is important as Christ and not as Jesus; nor can we
exalt his manhood at the expense of his deity. There are too
many "lives" of Jesus which give no insight into his nature

[2] See *Doctrine in the Church of England*. New York: Macmillan, pp.
74–75.

from the Christian point of view, and there are too many interpretations of the "living Christ" which give no indication that
he ever lived as a man.

The theological problem and the educational problem are
identical: it is the need to present Jesus as the Christ, historically conditioned as part of God's act of revelation and
eternally living in the bosom of the Father. The New Testament nowhere gives us a picture of Jesus as a "good man,"
although of course he was; but there is also no reference any-
where in the New Testament to a Christ who is not identified
with the historical Jesus.

The earliest Gospel, Mark, is not biography. It opens
abruptly: "The beginning of the Gospel of Jesus Christ, the
Son of God." The writer of Mark was not interested in Jesus
as a good man. He could not conceive of Jesus without adding
"Christ." There was no such thing for him as a "human" Jesus,
although Jesus was fully human to him. From the beginning it
was the faith of the Church that Jesus was the Lord, the
Christ, the anointed one. The earliest Christians were Jews,
and they were baptized in great numbers. The primitive baptismal creed was simply, "I believe that Jesus is the Messiah."
That was enough to mark off a Christian from his fellows, for
every Jew already believed in the God of the Old Testament.
This belief that Jesus was more than a prophet, more than a
teacher, more than a good man, meant risking one's Jewish
orthodoxy and even one's life. When non-Jews began to come
into the fold, the creed was expanded to say:

> "I believe in God, the Father,
> In Jesus Christ, his only Son,
> And in the Holy Spirit."

The motive power of this belief was enough to make men risk
the ire of the Roman emperor, being thrown to the lions,
suffering in prison, and other martyrdoms. No man ever died

for saying, "Jesus was a good man," but many men and women have suffered for claiming that Jesus Christ, who lived and died for our sins and rose again, is their Lord and Master. The Christian claim about Jesus Christ is a tremendous one. The Church has summed up its teaching about Jesus in two words: Incarnation and Atonement.

"God so loved the world" . . . "God was in Christ" . . . "The Word became flesh." Incarnation means simply "in the flesh." Jesus was not simply a man; he was also God in the flesh. God was in Christ. This is the Christian Gospel. At the same time, the emphasis upon flesh means that Jesus was completely human, but he was different from other men because God fully indwelt him. Thus, Jesus Christ becomes the object of our worship and the source of authority for our beliefs.

This was not an easy doctrine to establish, for there were many in the early Church who doubted or questioned this interpretation. The modern reader would assume that what they doubted was Jesus' deity, but that was not so. They asserted that Jesus was divine, but they were skeptical of his manhood. He only "seemed" to be a man, said some, as early as 100 A.D. And so the Fourth Gospel insisted that "the Word became flesh," and a later creed said, "became man." The insistence that Jesus was born and was tried and died and rose again, was to show his manhood.

The "good man" heresy is of late origin, and comes from the rise of the biographical interest. It is the usual emphasis of many "lives" of Jesus in our Church schools, and is just as dangerous as the opposite view which the early Church repudiated.

What we need to do in thinking of Jesus Christ is to begin at both ends at once. Jesus was a man, born of human parents, who lived and taught and suffered and died—just as Socrates or Buddha or Confucius did much the same in their day. But the Christian claim is that God was in Jesus in a unique way, and so we say Jesus was "God incarnate," God in humanity, God in the flesh. It is a paradox, with only a hyphen between God-man to help us.

What we find out, if we accept the paradox of starting at both ends and meeting ourselves at the middle, is that in Jesus Christ we have a revelation of what God is like. If Jesus Christ is "the way, the truth, and the life," then we have guidance in and from him, and we can pray, "let this mind be in you which was in Christ Jesus."

But God was in Christ for a reason. "God was in Christ," said St. Paul, "reconciling the world to himself." Thus, the fact that God was in Christ, which is "incarnation," is because God wanted something done, which is "atonement," by which God changed the relation between himself and men.

The "good news" of the Gospel is the reassertion that "God loved the world so much that he gave his only begotten Son, that whoever believes in him should not perish but have everlasting life." The promise of eternal life comes from God through Christ.

The background for this claim is found in the Old Testament. Yahweh entered into an agreement with Israel in Moses' time. There was a covenant between Yahweh and the people, a series of commandments. If the people kept these commandments, then Yahweh would be their God and lead them to the promised land. The first covenant was written in stone, and the Ten Commandments are basic to any religious morality. But it was an agreement between Yahweh and a nation, with no particular covenant with individuals. So there was a second covenant many years later, in which God's laws were written on the heart. Jeremiah put these words in Yahweh's mouth: "I will put my law within them, and will write it on their hearts; and I will be their God and they shall be my people" (Jer. 31:33b, G).

God has always wanted salvation for men, and in various ways it has been offered to men. God takes the initiative; he is the reconciler. And so one agreement was written in stone and another on men's hearts, and still it was not enough. A third covenant was necessary, written in blood. The prophets had already seen that a Messiah should come to redeem the nation of Israel. They knew that a day of the Lord would bring judgment upon them. They had sufficient hope to call out:

"Say to the daughter of Zion,
'See! Your salvation has come'" (Is. 62:11b, G).

They also knew the power of suffering, and that Israel must be a suffering servant. But they never saw the connection between the Messiah and the suffering servant. They did not know that God cared enough for man to take on his own shoulders the iniquity of us all.

So the third covenant came through suffering love, marked by the death of Christ. We repeat the heart of this at the words of institution for every celebration of the Lord's Supper, where Jesus' words are: "Drink ye all of this, for this is my Blood of the New Testament which is shed for you." "New Testament" is variously translated "new covenant" or "new agreement." This is the crux of the matter.

The covenant is not just the death of Christ, however, for it is the victory of the Cross in the resurrection which sealed the agreement for the disciples. It is Jesus Christ risen from the dead who is the living Christ. It was the resurrection experience, however it may be interpreted, which changed the disciples into the courageous men who acted to bring about the formation of the primitive Church. No story of the work of Jesus is complete without this final victory.

What a difference this made is evident in the history of the Church. Out of Jesus' mission came a little band of disciples which grew into a community of faithful people, spreading the Gospel throughout the known world. The Christian Church is a fact of our experience, centering in Jesus Christ. Wherever this belief in Jesus Christ has vanished, the Church has lost its power. Wherever men have believed in Jesus Christ, the Church has been a strong influence for good, and works of salvation have been wrought in Christ's name.

There is no mistaking this central element in the Gospel. The impact of Jesus Christ on history was enough to change the direction of history, and we say "B.C." and "A.D." There is "the year of our Lord" but there is no "A.J." or "after Jesus." There is no cult of Jesus the man as there might be a cult of John the Baptist or Socrates or Conan Doyle. This Church of ours is no archaic society in memory of a good man. This Church is "the Body of Christ," an extension of God's work in the world, and the Church brings us into the presence of the living Christ. For if God was in Christ, reconciling the world to himself, surely he is in his Church, fulfilling the promise of his third covenant which was marked by the death and resurrection of Christ.

So we see that the Christian religion is no easy morality. Christianity is not admiration of a good man who lived two thousand years ago. To be a Christian, one must have faith in Jesus Christ and belong to the Church which is the Body of Christ. There is simply no other Gospel than this: "the beginning of the good news of Jesus the Christ."

The Gospel means literally "good news," and it is just that. For the Gospel is news about God, telling us that God loves his creatures, whether they are sinners or not. God loves men so much that he enters the arena where they live and gives them commandments, and writes his law on their hearts, and (when this is not enough) he sends his only begotten Son, who is willing to suffer for men's sake. That is the kind of love God has for men, and surely that is good news.

To accept Jesus Christ as Lord and Savior, to be baptized in that faith, to follow Christ, to worship God every Sunday in his Church, and to work and pray and give for the spread of his kingdom—these are men's response to what God has already done for them in and through Christ. The path is open for men so that they can with confidence face every experience which life presses on them.

The New Testament knows no other religion than this. As man after man comes to faith in Jesus Christ and is baptized, his whole way of living is changed. Magicians and sorcerers, tax collectors and harlots, honest workers and dishonest politicians, high priests and simple housewives, rich and poor—they come under the preaching of Paul or Barnabas or Apollos, and they believe in Jesus Christ. They are brought into a new relationship with God through Jesus Christ, and they enter the life of the community, with its preaching, its sacraments, its care for widows and orphans, its concern for missionary work, and its care of the churches.

To these men and women, Jesus was a supremely good man, and they sought to be like him; but they did not try to take his place. He was truly *the* Son of God, as a first-born in a human family. So it was that men thought of themselves as "heirs of God, and joint-heirs with Christ." "Now are ye sons of God," says the Elder, "and it does not yet appear what ye shall be." "I call you no longer slaves but friends," says Jesus in the Fourth Gospel. Always Jesus takes the pre-eminent place, because he did the work of God in a unique way. "Our hope is that we may be as Jesus; not that we may be Christs." [3]

We are under a new covenant, a new dispensation, a new agreement, a new testament, which fulfills the promise of the Old Testament in a way which the prophets of old could never

[3] William Temple, *Doctrine in the Church of England.* New York: Macmillan, pp. 78–79.

conceive. To accept Jesus Christ as Lord and Savior means that "God was in Christ, reconciling the world to himself," and the world has never been the same since.

II

As we turn to the problem of teaching a sound Christology to children and young people in the curriculum of Christian education, we are faced with the issues which we have just discussed. There are many things which we need to do, but chief of them is to present Jesus Christ as an object of faith. This major aim need not obliterate other significant aspects, which include the winsomeness and attractiveness of Jesus as a human person, a full use of critical scholarship in presenting the Gospel story, and the proper use of age-group characteristics as a basis for the selection of material.

One of the major problems of Christian education is the place of the crucifixion in the curriculum. In a remarkable book called *Towards the Conversion of England*, there is this paragraph:

"Young people, particularly, of our humane age, are scandalized at the Scriptural emphasis on the inevitability of the Crucifixion, and at the Church's insistence in 'dragging it in' and giving it such prominence. This repugnance to the idea of the sacrifice of the Cross, as something horrible and revolting, represents a regression to the old pagan worship of the beautiful—the pagan unwillingness to face the ugly. . . . But there *are* ugly things in life, and they do not cease to be so because we refuse to face them. They can only be removed by coming down to them and dealing with them, in the spirit of the physician or the soldier. That spirit we all admire. The Cross is the ultimate expression of that heroic spirit. It is God entering the lists of sacrifice. If he refused this, he could not embody the highest good. The martyr, the doctor, the soldier would be higher than he. The Cross can only be understood in terms of sacrifice." [4]

With sacrifice rather than defeat or horror as the basis for presenting the crucifixion, it is possible to get at the heart of the Christian faith at an earlier age. There are difficulties with younger children who think of heroes as always victorious, but even this can be worked out when it is seen that the sacrifice of the Cross was followed by the victory of the resurrection.

The focal point of Christian faith need not be lost with any age-group. Naturally, the emphases will differ with the age and experience of the learner. It is possible to misuse almost any material, depending upon the leader's understanding of the total educational situation. A story is told of a missionary who held his primitive congregation enraptured with the story of the crucifixion, and his listeners could hardly stop asking for details. The missionary was thrilled with their intelligent grasp of the whole problem until the next day, when six members of an opposing tribe were found neatly crucified.

The basic approaches will include Jesus as a man, the sacrifice of the Cross and the Resurrection, the coming of the Church, and the Church's faith in Jesus Christ as Lord and Savior.

In the kindergarten and primary departments, the tendency is to stress the "baby Jesus," but this can be overdone both by its one-sided emphasis and by the repetition of the same stories until the children are bored. Only a few stories about Jesus can be related to the little child's experience and these need to be carefully selected. The process of Christian nurture is long and slow, and the Gospels were written for mature people, so we must not be impatient.

Certain imaginative stories about Jesus as a boy and a man will help greatly at this age-level. Such a book as John Oxen-

[4] *Towards the Conversion of England.* Westminster: Press and Publications Board of the Church Assembly, p. 2.

ham's *The Hidden Years* may be used with almost every age-group, while Dorothy Kunhardt's *Once There Was a Little Boy* is especially helpful at the ages of five and six. There are going to be unpredictable and sometimes profound questions asked by small children. It is here that often the relevance of theology will be most significant. It is in the actual teaching situation that theology will arise, and the resources of the mature faith of the teacher will be called upon for an answer that matches what the question means to the one who asks it. Depending on the capacity of the learner, the following question may come at any age from seven to twelve, and even later: "What is the difference between God and Jesus? Sometimes the minister begins a prayer to God and the next time to Lord Jesus. How many Gods are there anyhow?" This is an invitation to a discussion of the Trinity with older learners, but on the primary level it would have to be answered simply: "We believe that God is in Jesus, and because God is in us, too, he answers our prayers."

With juniors, much of the biographical material about Jesus as found in the Gospels may be used. The emphasis should be on his heroic stature, and on the changes he wrought in his listeners and disciples by the power of his personality. Opinions will vary as to how much of this should be in terms of the miraculous. Always, however, it should be kept in the forefront of the discussion that Peter and the others among the Twelve recognized him as the Messiah. If the picture of Jesus as a hero is strongly enough developed, this viewpoint will carry even this group through the sacrifice of the Cross and the victory of the Resurrection. They can understand that

> "The Church's one foundation
> Is Jesus Christ our Lord,"

and in the Christmas carols the high Christology of the various stanzas can have great teaching value. There will be some skepticism in this group, but it will not be hard to answer their questions. Again, the theological resources and the imagination of the leader will determine the success of inculcating the beginnings of a faith in Christ.

Most lessons for juniors and intermediates fall into the trap of presenting Jesus as a good man. It is a sound method of teaching, but often it leaves the learner with no insight into the faith of the Church about Jesus Christ. One way of overcoming this defect is to study the effect of faith in Christ on heroes of the Church, both in the past and present. Then it is necessary to go beyond this (or perhaps start with this) and find elements in daily life which make a difference because one is a Christian. The answer to this question should take on three aspects: it should provide a perspective for looking at the facts of life, it should change one's character, and it should enrich one's fellowship within the Church.

Let us use a sixth-grader as an example. He is eleven years old and therefore has not made his profession of faith or been confirmed or partaken of the Lord's Supper. His life in the congregation has been restricted to junior Church, an interesting church school class, and membership in one of the youth groups. He may have sung in the junior choir or assisted in some other way in worship. He knows a few facts about the characters of the Old Testament, is vague about Paul, and knows that Jesus liked children. He has typical boyish interests in Boy Scouts, his allowance, his swimming or skating or music lessons, and in group games with his friends after school. He tolerates his public school teacher and does well enough with his studies. What is the relevance of Christology for him? We might ask him: "Johnny, what does faith in Christ change in you during the week?"

"Gee, I don't know. He was swell to people, and maybe if I think about him I don't try to cheat Jim in marbles."

"It rained yesterday, and I guess you couldn't play baseball."

"It knocked our game out all right; but you know what! Mom was cleaning out the cellar, and I pitched in and helped her a lot."

"It's always good to help our Moms."

"Yea. But your lesson last Sunday helped me think of doing it. You told us how Jesus washed his disciples' feet, and I figured if a fellow like him would do that for his friends maybe I could try and help Mom more. . . . And you should 'a seen one of Jesus' parables work out at Joe's house the other night. Jim went right to the head spot at the table, and Joe's Mom had to tell him to move down the table."

There is nothing particularly profound about these statements, but they point to the relevance of Christian teaching on a boy's level. They are illustrated primarily in the development of character, for his fellowship in the Church is necessarily limited and his world-view is still elementary.

Most Churches customarily expect a profession of faith or confirmation at the age of twelve. This leads to great intellectual difficulties, for the average twelve-year old cannot understand most of the catechisms and other material which are the basis of instruction. The catechism is true but often irrelevant, and is usually taught without too much reference to the young person's experience. The language is frequently too technical and condensed, and even a good teacher cannot always relate such material to the areas of communication and experience of his learners. Yet it is just such theological information which is essential to the maturing Christian.

There are several alternatives. One is to fall back on material-centered teaching and to be satisfied with lip-service in terms of memory. A second is to postpone confirmation to a later age, which has many recommendations including, besides better understanding, a higher percentage of confirmations that are permanent in terms of loyalty to the Church. A third alternative is a serious attempt to restate the basic doctrines in language and concepts which a twelve-year-old will understand and make these ideas relevant to his experience. This is a difficult task. The basic article of faith is the acceptance of Jesus Christ as Lord and Savior.

The following approach has been used, with modifications, with twelve-year olds, high school students, and adults. It provides a pattern for an approach to Christology which begins with the human horn of the dilemma and attempts to transcend the gap of the hyphen in Jesus-Christ.[5] At any age, there is the recognition of Jesus as completely human. As we study the record of his life in the Synoptic Gospels, we are impressed by his kindness, his courage, his sympathetic healing, his righteous indignation concerning the evils of his day, in his fellowship with the down-trodden. Then we see another quality coming out in Jesus, the power to see potentialities in those with whom he comes in contact. At first, we can see this is such people as the despised tax collector, the harlot, the Samaritan, and rich young ruler, and many others. And then we see this power going beyond the Gospels, as the living Christ touches a Paul or a St. Francis of Assisi or a Horace Bushnell, and finally we come to see how Christ today draws out this same spirit in an Albert Schweitzer or in you or me. So we decide that pictures of Jesus with a halo about his head are not absurd art but an attempt to get at the meaning of Jesus for mankind. Jesus caused that kind of response in the Gospel stories, and his disciples recognized him as someone sent especially from God to be the Messiah, the Christ. Jesus is *the* Son of God, while all men are or can become sons of God. "We may become like him, but only *through* him." And still we are only beginning our exploration of the meaning of Jesus Christ. When we look at what happened to history

[5] See my *What We Can Believe*. New York: Scribners, pp. 89–94; my *The Challenge of the Church*. New York: Morehouse-Gorham, student's book, pp. 22–23, leader's manual, pp. 34–36.

because of the man Christ Jesus, we discover that in giving us the epochs of B.C. and A.D. he is the most important single fact of our whole civilization. The life, death, and resurrection of Jesus Christ made possible a new relationship (an at-one-ment) between God and man. Jesus has revealed the *way* of salvation and died to show it to us—which means that through faith in him we are committed to what our loving Father wants us to do in every act and thought. The final step is the hardest to comprehend, for while we can understand how God sent Jesus to do this for us, we still need to see what it means to say that God was in Jesus, that Jesus was God "in the flesh." "The Word became flesh and dwelt among us" means that in Jesus God was present as much as he can be in a human being, that he was "in Christ reconciling the world to himself."

These are the steps in theology, which various age-groups can follow with some degree of comprehension, but the act of faith is more than acceptance of belief. Faith is trust. No educational procedure can provide what only the grace of God can give, and sometimes this grace will come without full understanding. We are "justified" or "made upright" by faith. Careful use of such hymns as "O Jesus, I have promised to serve thee to the end," or "There is a green hill far away," or "Master of eager youth" may assist the process.

Profession of faith in Jesus Christ as Lord and Savior is usually followed by reception of Holy Communion. The sense of the presence of the living Christ associated with this sacrament is the final step toward full membership in the Church. But the educational process does not control the effect at this point. There is no guarantee that the worshiper will find Christ at any service of worship. There is no control of the degree of his faith or trust. The educational process may assist in providing information, nurture, and fellowship, but the contagion of the process in developing faith must be left in the hand of God. And as faith grows, more education will be required. One of the great errors of the Churches has been the assumption that faith will grow without the continuing process of nurture, but this can never be taken for granted. The fundamental law of learning is *experience*, and second only to it is *repetition*. Faith can be strengthened only as one repeats the learning process in relation to the new experiences of everyday life. Therefore, the absence of the adolescent boy or girl from the Church's educational process is dangerous, for without the continuing education of the Christian he ceases to know what he stands for. The need for the education of adults immediately becomes obvious in this connection. So evangelism and education go hand in hand, and the end of education is conversion to faith in Christ, and because neither faith nor education is static there is a continuous interrelation between the two.

The end result of faith in Christ which is assisted by the educational process has its roots in the earliest teaching of a child, even before Church school has any influence at all. We are more aware than ever before that the basic attitudes of character and personality and faith are developed by influences in the home from the beginning of a child's life. There is no content here which would satisfy a theologian, and yet basic attitudes inculcated by parents develop, as the child grows, into beliefs about the world and society around him. It is for this reason that neither public school nor Church ever has control of the educational situation, for the parents have a lengthy opportunity from the beginning. This accounts for many of the difficulties presented to leaders in school or Church and for the great variety of religious appreciation as children become old enough to receive the educational assistance of the Church prior to their acceptance of Jesus Christ.

The ultimate factor in the Christian educational process cannot be controlled by that process, for the gift of the grace of God comes in mystery. The educator makes ready a situation in which the grace of God may be received with intelligence and hope, but there is a permanent "Advent" season in Christianity which is beyond any methodology, or theory, or theology.

Thus, faith in Christ as Lord, which is the focal point of the Christian educational philosophy, is determined in the last analysis by factors which cannot be brought under control. The act of God and the man's response of faith are in an organic interpersonal relationship which grows out of the educational process but which cannot be guaranteed by it.

The relevance of this faith in Christ is found in the fruits of Christian living, and from this focal point of Christian education can be traced the many results of this faith. Here again the educational process is of supreme importance in guiding Christians toward maturity in their everyday living. As we turn to later chapters, these aspects will be discussed in detail.

CHAPTER THREE

THE SOURCE

THE educational philosophy which we are outlining insists on the relevance of Christian theology. The main task is to teach the truth about God, with all the implications arising from God's nature and activity, in such a way that the learner will accept Jesus Christ as Lord and Savior, will become a member of the Body of Christ, and will live in the Christian way. Parents and teachers must never lose sight of this fundamental goal, even with the youngest children.

The fundamental truth of the Christian revelation is unchanging; the good news given us in Christ Jesus is not altered by the ongoing process of history; there is a faith (but not a theology) given once for all to the saints. The presentation of this Gospel changes with succeeding generations and cultures, and our task is to present the truth about God to a particular people under specific conditions, which vary from culture to culture and from generation to generation and from age-group to age-group.

I

The source of all truth and hope is God himself, revealed to us by his mighty acts in history. While our fullest knowledge of God is given us in Christ, there is much truth about him that may come to any mind that is open and alert. The traditional arguments for the existence and nature of God, for example, do not come from the Bible but find their origin in the rational minds of the Greek philosophers. These arguments are never conclusive until they are combined with a "will-to-believe" and an act of faith, but they point in the direction of acceptance of God as the only adequate explanation of a rational universe. Only God gives us a basis for belief in a universe which makes sense, has purpose, and is moral. Only God can provide an explanation for the meaning of experience in prayer and worship, in sacrificial living, in love, and in our ability to live by the highest we know. Such knowledge of God as this is available to philosophers, to adherents of other religions, and to anyone who thinks seriously about the meaning of life. It is the fruit of what Thomas Aquinas called "natural theology," but it is not enough.

We are the inheritors of a specific revelation in Christ which is the culmination of the acts of God in history as recorded in the Old Testament and as kept alive for us in the traditions of the Church. It is a fact of human experience that Christians are a "peculiar people," with their special revelation in Christ that supersedes all other revelations. The door of revelation is not closed, for the living Christ is part of our everyday environment; but the direction of revelation is settled for us.

The Christian revelation is not concerned with the rational arguments for the existence of God and does not go back to considerations of First Cause, the nature of Being, or the evidence from Purpose. As a matter of fact, the Jewish-Christian tradition assumed these arguments and easily assimilated them when it came into contact with Greek culture; but the starting point is different.

Yahweh, in the Old Testament, is Lord of history, at work in the processes of development of the nation of Israel. As we follow the teachings of the Law and the Prophets, it becomes more and more evident that God is at work at the level where his people live, in their national catastrophes and racial ideals, in the moral law and in social justice, in the promise of salvation and in the threat of judgment. There are the covenants written in stone and in the heart, which lead finally to a covenant written in blood. God is active, personal, loving, just, and concerned with his people.

It is against this Jewish background of the God of the prophets that the New Testament revelation is to be understood. More and more we find that the idea of God as Father predominates, for the analogy of Fatherhood covers most of the attitudes which God has shown toward his people. God is personal and self-conscious, intelligent and purposeful, good and just and loving, and capable of communication and communion with human persons. He has none of the limitations of human personality, and yet he has all the qualities which make him supremely personal.

The most important thing about God is that he is the Father of Jesus Christ. It is in the love of God revealed in Christ that we have a clue to how God can be all-powerful and all-good at the same time. God is the only Father who can have absolute power without sacrificing his goodness; and this is because God is different from men, and his power is a different kind of power. It is not a power that suppresses or destroys; God's power gives life. God's power is not an imposition of his will on men's wills. God has the power to destroy, but he does not use it in that way unless judgment is necessary after love has been denied by men. God's power is always qualified by mercy, by love, by the offer of forgiveness.

Absolute power can be trusted only when there is also absolute love, and God's power is love in action—not force in action. God's all-powerfulness is expressed at the very point where men's will-to-power fails. God gave man freedom, with no strings attached, and God is powerful enough to take the consequences. In his love, he lets man choose his destiny; and in his power, he endures anything that man may inflict upon him. This is his power: his ability to give unreservedly, to make man independent of God so that man may become truly dependent upon God.

This is what we desire from a perfect Father. He gives his children every opportunity to choose their own destiny, with perfect freedom, providing help when asked but otherwise granting autonomy to his children as they become mature. And the price which God pays is in terms of suffering. God suffers as men suffer, supremely on the Cross, but always in the crosses of daily life. "The Cross," says D. R. Davies, "is the historic symbol of God's omnipotence, of his infinite capacity to endure any and every evil that man can perpetrate, so that, through the endurance of it all, men will, at long last, achieve their freedom in willing dependence upon God. . . . God endures every pain, every horror, every tragedy, every sin —and, in spite of it all, does not crush freedom." [1]

This God of the Christian revelation, whose power is love even to the death of his Son on the Cross, is not a soft, sentimental, romantic deity who pampers his children. The opposite is true. In giving men freedom, he endowed them with responsibility, and responsibility means taking the consequences of one's acts. God may use a velvet glove, but his fist is of iron. Opposition to God wreaks havoc, for men's lives can be demolished against God's resistance. God is holy and sovereign, and is the only Person good enough and powerful enough and loving enough to be the Source of all that we are or may be.

The Christian truth about God as Father is only one aspect of his nature, just as his revelation of himself in Jesus Christ is another. Too often these two are not placed in proper perspective, and even more often the third element in the Chris-

[1] *Down Peacock Feathers.* New York: Macmillan, pp. 30, 33.

tian picture of God is lost altogether. Many modern Christians are like the early disciples in Ephesus, of whom Paul asked:

> " 'Did you receive the Holy Spirit when you became
> believers?'
> 'No,' they said to him, 'we never even heard that
> there was a Holy Spirit' " (Acts 19:2, G).

Today's Christian has heard that there is a Holy Spirit, but too frequently his knowledge is summarized in the Apostles' creed: "I believe in the Holy Ghost, *period*." The basic meaning is simple: the God who made us and who was present in Christ has always been with us. God is Spirit and indwells us. The traditional gifts of the Holy Spirit are summarized in a prayer at confirmation:

> "Daily increase in them thy manifold gifts of grace: the
> spirit of wisdom and understanding; the spirit of counsel
> and ghostly strength, the spirit of knowledge and true
> godliness, and holy fear." [2]

This is a fully rounded description of what God the Holy Spirit does for us. He is the source of all our knowledge and power. From him comes the "light of the everlasting Gospel," mixed with the "gumption" or understanding which directs our insights into practical channels. We speak also of the Holy Spirit as God's counsel, for our decisions are helped when we meditate upon them in terms of "the mind of Christ," when we ask "what thou wouldst have us to do." And still nothing happens without power, which the prayer quaintly calls "ghostly strength." When the Holy Spirit is called the "Comforter," we need to remember that "comfort" means to cheer, revive, encourage, invigorate, refresh, or strengthen. Too often, however, religious devotion ends up against the blank wall of

[2] *The Book of Common Prayer*, p. 297.

an irrelevant idealism, and it is by the action of the Holy Spirit
that we obtain knowledge of the facts and are defended
from error.

This is never an easy-to-take immanentism. God is at work
within us, and this leads to the experience of "true godliness,"
which carries us to God-beyond-us. This results in "holy fear."
The psalmist says that "the fear of the Lord is the beginning
of wisdom." This does not mean fear in the sense of dread or
fright or terror; we are not afraid of God; what is meant is
that God is so great, so powerful, so good, so loving, so near—
that we fall on our knees in his presence.

> "God himself is with us;
> Let us all adore him,
> And with awe appear before him." [3]

The Christian revelation about God is summarized in the
doctrine of the Trinity. Whereas it is not too difficult to conceive of Jesus Christ as the focal point of God's Word, with
God as Father and Holy Spirit also in the picture, when we
think of them as three and as one at the same time, we run
into trouble. This has always been so. We can take solace in
the statement of Augustine:

"Why then do we not call these three together one person,
as we call them one being or one God? Why do we say three
persons, while we do not say three Gods or three beings, unless
it be that we desire some one word to serve for the meaning
whereby the Trinity is understood, so that when we say there
are three, and people ask us, 'Three what?' we need not be
altogether silent?

"When the question is asked, 'Three what?' human language labors under great poverty of speech. The answer is
given, however, 'Three persons,' not that it might be expressed,
but that it might not be left unexpressed.

[3] *The Hymnal,* 1940. No. 477.

"When then it is asked what the three are, or who the three are, we betake ourselves to the finding out of some special or general name under which we may embrace these three; and no such name occurs to the mind, because the preëminence of divinity surpasses the power of customary speech. For God is more truly thought than he is uttered, and exists more truly than he is thought." [4]

Certainly the word "person," as relating to the Trinity, does not have the meaning which is denoted today in common speech. Persons in the Trinity are "half-way between nouns and adjectives. If they are 'aspects,' they are eternal and are as it were relatively distinct and diffcrent; if they are 'persons,' they are so interpenetrating and so make up the one life which is God that they are also one together." [5]

The doctrine of the Trinity is a fundamentally sound and enduring attempt to translate the richness of men's experience of God into abstract terms. While it is bound to be unsatisfactory in some ways, it has served to protect the Christian heritage from various heresies and variations which would have emasculated the power of Christian faith.

Without assuming that the following is a complete statement of the nature of the Triune God, let us seek a simple outline of his meaning for us today.[6] A summary which appears in some catechisms is that the creed teaches this:

"First, I learn to believe in God the Father, who hath made me, and all the world.
Secondly in God the Son, who hath redeemed me, and all mankind.

[4] On the Trinity, V, 10. Quoted by John W. Moment in We Believe. New York: Macmillan, pp. 16–17.
[5] W. Norman Pittenger, Christ and Christian Faith. New York: Round Table, p. 139.
[6] See my Religion Makes Sense. Chicago: Wilcox and Follett, 1950, pp. 228–235.

Thirdly, in God the Holy Ghost, who sanctifieth me, and all the people of God,

And this Holy Trinity, One God, I praise and magnify, saying,

Glory be to the Father, and to the Son, and to the Holy Ghost;

As it was in the beginning, is now, and ever shall be, world without end. Amen."

First of all, God made me. I am his child and belong to him. This is God's first gift, that I am loved by God. No matter what happens to me or to the world, I am his and this is his world. I have security and love and hope, because God made me and all the world.

Every Christian child learns this. He is baptized, and this symbolizes his being born into God's family. He is taught that this is God's world, in terms that he can understand. He learns about the birds and the bees, because little minds can grasp these facts. Jesus emphasized this with his teachings about the lilies of the field and the sparrows with their nests. And if God cares for these, how much more does he love you, O ye of little faith? God as Creator put resources into the world for men to use. Farmers see God's creative power in the growth of a plant; doctors see the power of God in the mystery of healing; social scientists see God's power in the breaking down of barriers between nations; scientists see God's creative might in atomic power. The creation of the world, with all its resources and all its possibilities, is God's gift to men.

Secondly, I learn to believe in God the Son. God does not leave us without help. He did not give us a world as a toy to destroy. He provided the power to turn men from their evil ways. To redeem means literally "to buy back." The early Church put this dramatically by saying the children of God were kidnapped by the Devil and had to be ransomed. The only price the kidnapper would accept was God's own Son, and God loved his children enough to sacrifice Christ as a ransom for many. The price of our sins was so high that none of us could pay it, only the Father through his Son. This is a poetic way of putting the problem, but the price was that high.

This idea of redemption is at the center of the Christian faith. The gift of redemption is already given, just as the gift of creation is already given. The problem is, how are we to get God's gift, and this is the focal point of the Christian religion. The Church exists for this purpose, which is why we call the Church the Body of Christ. Man cannot buy or earn salvation, but he can accept it. Christian salvation is easier than earning it by merit, because all that is needed is faith and repentance; but it is harder, because faith and repentance involve the giving of the total self to God and asking God for power to do his will rather than man's.

Finally, then, I believe in God the Holy Ghost. To sanctify means "to make holy." God not only creates man and makes it possible for man to be forgiven, he also helps man at every stage in his spiritual pilgrimage. God gives men strength to do his will. Sometimes it comes directly, as when man faces a spot decision and is overwhelmed with a sense of direction from above; again, he finds latent resources in himself which are brought to the fore in a crucial moment or when the way is long and hard; normally, it is simply the sense that God is with a man in following God's will in daily living.

The gifts of God are threefold, and these gifts reveal the nature of the Triune God in his relevance to our human situation. It is something which is very simple and fundamental, and yet it can become involved in all the complexities of ethical decisions.

The Christian God in all his richness leads us to a paradox. When we speak of one of the members of the Trinity, Father, Son, or Holy Spirit, we refer to that "person" as "he" and not "it," but when we speak of the Triune God we also say "he" and not "they." The truth about God must be seen from two sources at once. As D. M. Baillie suggests, theologians tend to think about the distinctive nature of God from two points of view. One approach is through the teachings of Jesus, Paul, John, and the rest of the New Testament, which gives us the character of God; the other is through the development of the idea of the Trinity. This double approach gives a picture of a God who does what we know God has done! It provides a basis for accepting the dictum: "I . . . yet not I, but the grace of God." [7]

II

When we come to the problems of teaching the meaning of God to boys and girls, there are obvious difficulties. We need to recall, first of all, that the mysteries of abstract thinking are a closed book to most young people until they are ready for their first course in the history of philosophy; and we need to remember also that historical processes do not begin to make sense to boys and girls until they are about twelve. For those under twelve, then, the approach to the meaning of God will be primarily in terms of actual experiences of God at work; for those over twelve, the emphasis will be on God as he revealed himself in history and today; while for those beyond high school there is the approach through philosophical ideas.

But this does not mean that the Trinity is to be ignored until we approach it philosophically. The early Church came to the meaning of the Trinity through experience, and not through either history or philosophy. With the wrong approach, however, we are likely to come up against the diffi-

[7] See D. M. Baillie, God Was in Christ. New York: Scribners, pp. 143–5; all of ch. vi is significant. For another approach, cf. Leonard Hodgson, Doctrine of the Trinity. New York: Scribners.

culties listed by Marguerite Harmon Bro. She tells of a minister's son, aged twelve, who visited a Jewish Reformed
Synagogue and heard the Jewish teacher explain some of the
differences between Judaism and Christianity. In surprise
and wonder he hurried home and called to his mother:

"Mother, did you ever hear about the Three-in-One?"

"Did I ever hear of what? Come up here!"

Horace bounded upstairs: "Did you ever hear about the
Three-in-One—Father, Son, and Holy Ghost, blessed Trinity,
in one Godhead?"

"Why, Horace," replied his mother, "you've heard of the
Trinity all your life."

"Not until this morning. Mr. Levy told the boys—" [8]

Horace discovered the Trinity in the life situation of comparing the Jewish and Christian concepts of God. The complexities of theology, and especially the vocabulary surrounding
it, are a closed book to most youngsters of twelve. They may
be able to repeat the creeds and the catechisms, but usually it
is pure verbalization until light suddenly dawns. The difficulty
for most of us, even though we have mastered fundamental
ideas about the Christian God, is to alter our adult and technical vocabularies sufficiently to express the basic ideas in
Basic English.

The purpose is relatively simple. If the Triune God is true
we can find evidences of him at work in the experiences of a
child as well as of an adult. If our task is to teach the truth by
leading the learner into the discovery of the truth for himself,
we can set up the conditions whereby he may grow in grace.
To state this is much easier than to accomplish it, for we
come up against the fact that "no man hath seen God at any
time" and thus we must find God in his handiwork.

A group of children were discussing their Thanksgiving
turkey.

[8] *When Children Ask.* New York: Harpers, pp. 31–32.

"We should thank Mother for cooking this wonderful turkey," said Jane.

"We ought to thank Dad for buying it," said Paul.

"And the farmer for growing him," said Bill.

"But don't we thank God for it?" asked Sue.

"Where would God be without Mom and Dad and the farmer?" asked Bill.

"And where would they be, and the turkey, too, without God?" answered Sue. "God makes everything grow."

On a more elementary level, Mary Alice Jones records a conversation between Bobby and his mother. Bobby had planted a radish that did not grow because Bobby had not watered it. Bobby is annoyed because God had not watered his garden, because God can do anything. Finally, his mother asks:

" 'Do you think it would be a good plan if he did? If he treated you as if you were baby Mary who has to have everything done for her?' "

" 'I would not like to be treated like the baby,' Bobby decided. 'I should have remembered to water my garden.' " [9]

Young children are going to have many erroneous ideas about God, such as his location in the sky. If they are taught this by teachers and parents, or by poorly worded hymns, they will lose faith in their sources of information when they learn better. If, however, they are merely testing their own false concepts, they will seek further for a satisfying answer. The teacher must have a sufficiently sound theology not to give wrong answers to questions, and must have an adequate knowledge of the learners so as not to be satisfied with verbalization.

The type of questions about God which arise in the mind of a five year old are given in Ruth Davis Perry's *Children Need Adults*. They have serious geographical problems, for God makes it rain and is inside of you at the same time. They are aware of God's presence in the silence. They feel secure

[9] *Tell Me About God.* Chicago: Rand, McNally, p. 43.

because of God's love and cannot understand it when they fall out of a swing. They throw balls in the air but not too high because God might catch it and not throw it back. When a puppy dies, they want to die, too, so they can play with the puppy; but they do not understand that they could not come back and play with Daddy. At this period, most growth in religious concepts and attitudes must arise from actual questions, for any attempt to go beyond the "growing edge" will only add to the confusion. But questions can be stimulated by the right kind of answers and thus the child can be led to his own ability to answer his own questions.

With this age, nature, home, and kindergarten will each contribute to the widening horizon of the child's knowledge. There are all the experiences of birds and bees and worms, of plants and gardens, of Christmas and Easter rituals in the home, of grace at meals and evening prayers, of adjustment to the class at Church school. And God is at work in the least of all these children.[10]

With the fourth or fifth grader, the approach should be primarily through the lives of great heroes of past and present, tying in the laws of sportsmanship and goodness. The heroic stature of men and women in whom God is at work can be deeply appreciated. The emphasis is not on history but on the contemporary value of such persons for the decisions that juniors must make today. Many different approaches are possible, for there are the great heroes such as Francis of Assisi whose love for animals surpassed that of any modern Boy Scout; there are missionaries who have carried the story to all corners of the world, and there are those who have cleaned up communities with all the verve of Old Testament prophets. To discover that the "way of good will" is based on the message of "peace to men of good will" is to grow in faith and character.

[10] See *Children Need Adults*. New York: Harpers, pp. 112–136.

One of the modern hymns which junior boys and girls love begins with,

"I sing a song of the saints of God"

and it ends with this remarkable stanza:

"They lived not only in ages past,
There are hundreds of thousands still,
The world is bright with the joyous saints
Who love to do Jesus' will.
You can meet them in school, or in lanes, or at sea,
In church, or in trains, or in shops, or at tea,
For the saints of God are just folk like me,
And I mean to be one, too." [11]

They also appreciate "The Son of God goes forth to war," "Remember all the people who live in far off lands," and "In Christ there is no East or West." This reflects their own experiences and brings God to the level of their own existence. They are just beginning to understand history, but God at work in historical processes is still beyond them. The need of the leader for a mature view of God is necessary, however, if answers to questions are not to be misleading.

The major problem faces the teacher and pastor at the level of confirmation. The limitations of the twelve year old, in the seventh grade, are very pronounced when it comes to knowledge about God. Emotionally, he may be ready for the full fellowship of Christian worship, but intellectually he is far short of understanding what the various churches expect him to know.

One of the best examples of instruction along this line is *Creative Thinking on the Creed*, by William Grime.[12] He

[11] Lesbia Scott, by permission Morehouse-Gorham Co. *The Hymnal*, 1940, No. 243.
[12] Published by Department of Christian Education of the Diocese of Long Island, 170 Remsen St., Brooklyn. Quoted by permission.

records the discussions of a class of nine boys and twelve girls, mostly fourteen years old. In the first session, after careful consideration of the Apostles' creed, which all of them knew as part of their worship, the following comments were made in written form:

"You are making promises to believe in God the Father Almighty, but I would like to know how God created the world, the planets and atoms."

"Does science believe that God has been made up?"

"I cannot say I've had experience with God."

"We pledge to a picture of Christ when we say this at worship service, but when shall I know that it's true?"

"Hell has always bothered me. Do you think it should be in here? For, if a good person like Jesus went to Hell, then we are all going there."

"This is a pledge you believe in God as the Maker of all things like peoples' minds and people themselves."

"You have to put your faith in something but, if I think too much about the Holy Ghost and God, I get a conglomeration."

This is the level at which the students began (and they were at least two years older than many confirmation classes). The leader helped them by sketching in some historical background, and then enlisted the cooperation of the whole class in writing a creed for themselves, not as a substitute for the creed as used in worship, but as an aid to understanding the symbol of their faith. They considered other creeds written for the same purpose.

They had no trouble with belief in God as Maker of heaven and earth, but "Ghost" reminded them of Hallowe'en and white sheets, and "descended into hell" meant "he comes into everybody's sorrows to help." As they came to the conclusion of ten weeks of intensive study of this one subject, all the pupils had an increased appreciation of the Apostles' creed and they had learned much more by rephrasing the creed for their own information than a casual perusal would indicate. Their own creed is appended here to show how fourteen year olds can think when working with a creative teacher who is trained in both theology and educational method.

"I believe (commit myself to) God the Father Almighty, Maker of heaven and earth, so I must worship Him, through Jesus Christ His only Son our Lord, Who came to this earth through the Holy Spirit and Mary, His mother, to show us what God is really like; how important we are as His children and how to live up to our best selves.

"I believe He showed and proved God's love for us by His teachings, healings, His crucifixion under Pontius Pilate and through His resurrection from the dead, after which He withdrew from the sight of men's eyes to stay with them as Guide and Helper in building His world family—His Holy Church.

"I believe God forgives our sins if we forgive others their sins.

"I believe He still comes into everybody's lives and sorrows, helping them to make right judgments.

"I believe in all good people who lived before Jesus Christ came, and those who have worked with Him as His friends, from the Apostles' time until now, to make God's kind of cooperation and kindness come true in all people. So I believe in working with Him, through His Church, to make a better world for everybody.

"I believe that when we have done God's will on earth, we go to be with Him for eternal life, joy and service. Amen."

We may not agree with the orthodoxy of some of these statements, but it shows what a grasp of Christian truth is possible for the fourteen year old mind under ideal teaching conditions. But it must be remembered that this class met for this purpose for ten successive Monday afternoons, and for every Sunday for six months for the remainder of their instruction, and that God became real to them in his fulness.

The upper high school and college student comes to the question of God's place in his life from a different perspective. He has a grasp of history, some knowledge of the Bible, and is being exposed to modern science, to secular assumptions about behavior, and to the growing pains of later adolescence. Here is the opportunity for appreciation of God at work in history, for an understanding of the meaning of revelation as "the coincidence of a particularly revealing event and a particularly appreciative mind," as William Temple defined it,[13] for insight into what Jesus Christ accomplished in changing history, for seeing the fulfilment of the religion of the prophets by the mission of Christ, for connecting the work of Jesus as the Christ with the Church as the Body of Christ. God as Father, Son, and Holy Spirit, while not understood in his fulness, becomes more than a formula.

But with the new knowledge which comes from modern science, the young people are becoming skeptical and are asking why and how this could have happened. History is not presented in most secular schools and colleges in such a way that an easy transition can be made to the understanding of God as Lord of history. The more abstract beliefs are not always presented by the Church so that they will stand against the assumptions of modern science. Here is a great challenge which depends mostly on the ability of the leader for creative leadership of discussions.

Some of the hymns on the Trinity will provide a basis for discussion, especially "Holy Father, great Creator," which describes the work of each "person," and "I bind unto myself today the strong Name of the Trinity" which is ascribed to St. Patrick.

The most effective approach even on this level is to find

[13] *Nature, Man and God.* New York: Macmillan, p. 315.

interpretations of experience today which lead to belief in the Triune God. We discover who God is by the study of his handiwork in nature, in history, in society, and in individuals. We need the perspective of God at work beyond us before we can understand what God has done for us.

But just as faith in Christ is the focal point and cannot be coerced, so faith in the Triune God comes ultimately from God's grace. The grace of God may work through the educational system if it is sufficiently evangelical, for ultimately the concern of evangelism is loyalty to the whole of God and service to him in the fellowship of his Church. But the Church through its educational procedures presents only the information and the challenge, and then it leaves the result in the hands of God. But, as should be evident by now, sound theological beliefs are relevant to the process of salvation, for beliefs become faith when they are accepted as guides to action, and our task as educators is to inculcate the truth of God's revelation in such a way that our learners will respond to God's promise of salvation through Christ and his Church.

If we do not know where we are going, creative teaching is dangerous in that it will lead to the denial of truth and the mutual exchange of ignorance; but if we know the truth which makes men free, we will in the freedom of creative teaching lead the learners to accept God's revelation as God speaks to them. That is why educational method must be grounded in theology, but also why theology is a tool and God is the center and goal of all our teaching.

CHAPTER FOUR
THE CREATURE

T HE trained teachers and parents are often aware of the
characteristics of the children, but it is equally important to know what these creatures are from the standpoint
of Christian doctrine, in order to give them knowledge of
themselves. There is need for a clear concept of the nature of
man, as illustrated perhaps in the learners themselves and certainly in the Christian revelation. Too often Christian teachings have emphasized one or another of the two sides of man's
nature, and we have had sin painted in such blackness that
man's inhumanity to man seems to summarize the whole story,
or we have seen such illustrations of goodness even among those
who "make mistakes" that man's sin has been denied. As an
illustration of the optimistic type, there was the writer who
commented that men were doing so many evil things that we
almost had to go back to the "absurd doctrine" of original sin.
The pessimistic approach on the other hand refuses to admit
even an "image" of God in which man was created, except by
the "myth" of the fall. A balanced view, as we shall see,
must include the paradoxical nature of man as a child of God
and as a sinner at the same time.

I

Man is a creature of God. Where man came from is not
important religiously, as long as God is the Creator. It is very

likely that man is the product of evolution, a process which has taken millions of years and which began perhaps as pictured in the "Rite of Spring" animations of the motion picture, *Fantasia*. The significant fact of history is that man, with all his paradoxical qualities which mark him off from the animals, appeared on earth as a creature of God and as a member of the animal kingdom.

The Genesis story tells in dramatic form how men came to disobey God and points to the common experience that all men have in them the tendencies of rebellion against God. It has been said that no mother of a child under six months old thinks Baptism is necessary, and no mother of a child over six months old believes that Baptism does any good. The fundamental qualities of sinfulness appears almost from the beginning of life, as soon as the tendencies have a chance to make themselves evident.

"Sin is not only individual wrong doing, whether by commission or omission. It is the fact, however brought about, of being 'off the right course.' The world has departed from the course for which it was created and has absorbed a basic principle of error into the whole direction of life. . . . Reconciliation with God can never be accomplished by man himself. . . . Every new good which he achieves brings with it its own peculiar evil. . . . Such is the tragic quality of man's fallen nature, which we term Original Sin." [1] This is the kind of world and society into which everyone is born.

It is possible to expand this description indefinitely. Sin is both individual and social, and collective guilt is even more destructive than individual guilt, although that does not mean any one has the right to confess his neighbor's sin, for every individual partakes of the fundamental disease of human society.

[1] *Towards the Conversion of England*, pp. 19, 29.

The fact that men are finite creatures has nothing to do with their sinfulness, for God created them finite. Man's sinfulness is his rebellion against God, and this comes chiefly in two ways. On the one hand, he accepts his affinity with the animal kingdom, and uses the powers (of reason and will) which God gave him to rise above the animal kingdom to sink below the level of the animal kingdom. The disreputable sins are primarily man's misuse of his animal nature, and these are frowned upon by most societies. For the Christian, however, these sins are so obvious that they automatically convict the sinner; and thus they are not so serious as the hidden sinfulness which appears with goodness.

The greatest exposure of pride and self-deception as sin given us in this century has been by Reinhold Niebuhr. It is when man seeks to become a superman, displacing God and using power to control other men, that he plants the seeds of self-destruction on both the individual and corporate level. The potentialities for goodness in man, which are obviously present, are corrupted by respectability and pride as illustrated in the much-maligned Pharisee, and this self-deception turns out to be other than the submission to the will of God which is true goodness. On an elementary level, a little girl saw this when she prayed: "Please God, make the bad people good, and the good people nice."

John C. Bennett brings out the paradox in man which should never be lost in our consideration of the nature of man. There is, he says, an Augustinian tradition which paints man as a sinner, with sin on every level of spiritual attainment; and this means that every form of Utopianism is an illusion; thus, we are brought up against the need for continuous repentance. But we must remember also that there is an essential goodness in man which is not destroyed when it is corrupted; man as a finite child of nature is a rational being, a free, creative and responsible self, who comes to himself in social relations. The truths of both Augustinianism and Liberalism are maintained in this series of propositions.[2]

This balanced view of man as a child of God and still a sinner, as able to achieve positive goodness in freedom and only by the grace of God, as seeking the kingdom and receiving it only from God, as in a tragic human situation and living the abundant life, as saved through the atonement of Jesus Christ and needing to be saved through repentance and commitment, as an individual and finding sanctuary in the Church, as loved of God and suffering God's judgment, is an anthropology which has developed from a profound and Biblical approach to man's present predicament.[3]

Here is a situation in which we see consecrated lives which seem to be in harmony with God's will. To such lives we sometimes ascribe perfection, although no Christian observer would ascribe perfection to himself. But usually closer examination will show that this perfection only appears on certain levels of behavior, and that the other levels illustrate various kinds of sin. What we come up against is that man cannot save himself by himself, and with all the strengthening power of the Holy Spirit he still does not stay on the narrow path which leads to salvation. A motor car in a ditch always needs to be pulled out, but once under way again it may still go into another ditch. Man's need of God's power is always evident.

Man's dependence upon God is for more than goodness, however. We thank God "for our creation, preservation, and all the blessings of this life," but we need God for all our troubles and sufferings and other evils which are not directly

---

[2] Cf. John C. Bennett, "The Christian Conception of Man," in David E. Roberts and Henry P. Van Dusen, eds., *Liberal Theology*. New York: Scribners, pp. 191–204.

[3] See my *Church and Organized Movements*, (New York: Harpers), p. 6, also *Christianity and the Contemporary Scene*, (New York: Morehouse-Gorham), pp. 11–12.

due to our own sins and sometimes are not due to the sins of humanity. "God is a very present help in trouble," and man needs him desperately in times of sickness and death as well as in times of temptation.

Man is never self-sufficient, and his claim to self-sufficiency is another form of self-deception. The problems of Christian living as such are to be postponed to a later chapter, but in this context we need to look at the "possibilities of Christian man."

If we take man seriously in his historical situation, we come to the realization that the process of salvation begins within history, eternal life begins now; but the Source of salvation and its realization are always beyond history. This has led to at least four emphases on the responsibilities of man within the historical process.

The first emphasis places man's citizenship unequivocally in heaven. This world is not worth saving and the only purpose of man is to accept his place in the heavenly kingdom which is promised him. This means that ethical endeavor and social action are irrelevant, except in so far as the "elect" behave as those already saved should behave. This is a refusal to take history seriously as an arena of God's work, with the exception of the Incarnation. Some types of Fundamentalism fall into this error, as does the extreme form of Barthianism.

A second emphasis takes history too seriously as having achieved God's will. It is an absolutizing of the relative, so that several illusions predominate the view of man. Foremost among those holding one or another variation of this position are the Utopians, who maintain that a perfect kingdom will be achieved on earth. While the illusion lasts, this view contains great motive power, but history destroys the vision and pessimism completes the circle. Many of the false idealisms of recent years, such as pacifism, isolationism, social reform, and others, have fallen into this trap. The Roman Catholics have their own version of this error, which is identifying the Church with the kingdom of God on earth. The secularists have their version, which is the illusion of progress. Christians, under the influence of evolutionary theories, have borrowed this interpretation of history, and then history refuted them.

A third view begins with the irrelevance of Christian ethics. No one could follow Jesus' teachings literally and live. Even he could not stand against the world. His teachings, therefore, are only applicable to the coming kingdom. When the kingdom comes by a divine act, men will be empowered to do God's will. A variation of this is that while Jesus expected the kingdom to come, his ethics were for the interim between his mission and the kingdom. Another variation is the Lutheran double standard, which applies Jesus' ethics to personal living but gives predominance to the various orders of society which are not bound by the personal ethics which Jesus taught.

The Christian doctrine of man makes it clear that man does not do the will of God, for he remains a sinner in God's sight no matter what he does. Reinhold Niebuhr therefore talks of the absolute ideal of love as an "impossible possibility." The relevance of an impossible ideal, however, is never made quite clear. The ideal that is held is so high that one loses sight of it in the problems of everyday living. When one does good, he knows it is still evil, and for many this paralyzes Christian moral effort at its source.

There is truth in all these theories which must be accounted for. The will of God is absolute, and in its transcendent nature cannot be achieved by creatures. But that is only part of the story. God's will is also expressed in time, for he is Lord of history. The Holy Spirit, whatever else he may be, is God immanent, at work in the world and in us. This does not lessen the absoluteness of his will, but it does make his will relevant to history and to men.

Men, living in the finite perspective of history, can align themselves with the processes which God has set in action, and in so doing they can *approximate* God's will for them. They do not achieve God's absolute will, but they are sensitive to the possibilities of value in each concrete situation, and thus they can act as channels through which God's will operates.

When men use all their abilities to know and to obey God's will, they still need the power which God may grant them in order to achieve it. The best they can hope for are sinless moments, for no man can remain absolutely obedient to God. The kingdom of God comes by God's act, for it is God's reign which is being established, and man fulfils his part as a creature.[4]

The destiny of man is more than being a faithful servant, for man is a citizen of two worlds. Those who insist that man is a citizen of heaven are right, just as those who see man as an historical creature are correct, for man lives in time and is made for eternal life. History never forgives, but Christian man experiences the forgiveness of God. There is always the hope of immortality, "for God created man for immortality" (Wis. of Solomon 2:23,G). The "testimony is that God has given us eternal life, and that this life is found in his Son" (I Jn 5:11,G).

So it is that man comes into the fellowship of the Church by faith, and becomes the recipient of God's grace, and thus he is enabled to overcome his sins and his fears, and enter into the peace which is beyond his understanding. In this community, he does not become sinless, but he is strengthened to approximate God's will for him because of his intention to achieve absolute commitment. He has assurance of what he hopes for and conviction about things not seen (Heb. 11:1), and he is made whole by faith. This is Christian maturity.

[4] See "The Relevance of Christian Ethics," *Religion in Life*, XIV:205-215, for a fuller treatment of this theme.

II

As we turn to the needs of the various age-groups, we discover that in approaching the Christian doctrine of man they are talking about themselves and their own experiences. In the process of growing up, adjusting to other persons, learning to live in a family and in the community, the children are actually demonstrating the nature of man, and thus teachers and parents have abundant illustrations in front of them all the time.

While the formal doctrines of original sin and the "image" of God will not be introduced as such among the youngest ones, it will be possible to build up attitudes which make possible an acceptance of a balanced view of man in their later thinking. What happens too often is that lessons for small children fall into the errors of the optimistic picture of man where all is sweetness and light, although there is one set of lessons which goes to the other extreme and presents the Genesis story of the Fall in the first grade without reference to the children's present-day experience. Both approaches are irrelevant.

Among the children in the first or second grades, we have their experiences of adjustment to group life in home and at school, at church and in the neighborhood, where they meet children and adults with varying moral and religious qualities. There is always someone who does not like children; there is frequently an alcoholic; there are various perverted people; and there are all those who are nice to the children. Children are taught not to accept rides with strange men or women, and a reason must be given. They know why we have policemen. As they grow, they learn to accept responsibilities on their own account, and they become aware of their own shortcomings in their perfectly normal failures to fulfil what is expected of them. They need security, and become sensitive to their dependence upon their parents and ultimately upon God. They know there is such a thing as death, but that God does not let the spirit die. They even can see the meaning, although they cannot understand the words, of Paul's statement: "I do not understand what I am doing, for I do not do what I want to do; I do things that I hate. . . . I do not do the good things that I want to do; I do the wrong things that I do not want to do. But if I do the things that I do not want to do, it is not I that am acting, it is sin, which has possession of men" (Romans 7:15, 19–20,G).

Such ideas may be expressed in prayers: "Bless, O God, my school. Bless my teachers and school fellows, and keep us all strong in body and soul. Help me to be unselfish, and especially kind to new boys and girls. Amen." Or in this:

> "Lord Jesus, when you as a boy
> Knelt by your bed at night,
> You trusted God would care for you
> In darkness and in light.
> So, as I kneel beside my bed,
> I'm glad you don't forget
> That you were once a little child;
> That children need you yet." [5]

A common question by an eight year old is, "Why are people bad?" It is not easy to answer, for the child knows that he wants to be good, although he readily admits that he does not succeed. It does not help much to be told, "You were born that way," although that is true. It is more helpful to let the child analyze his own behavior and try to see why he did what he did. He can use this self-understanding as a basis for analyzing the behavior of others among his friends and among

[5] Katherine Smith Adams, *Now We Are Going to School*. New York: Morehouse-Gorham, p. 73.

public officials whom he feels he knows through conversations, and thus he begins to have a Christian doctrine of man. He is curious about people in jails, about leaders of enemy countries, about friends whom he sees stealing and cheating and lying.

Sometimes between the ages of six and nine, there is the first real encounter with authority with rebellion as a real possibility. For the child to grow, there must be real freedom to reject authority. This is symbolized by the child striking his mother. From a psychological point of view, the child thereby wills his mother's death, although his existence depends upon her. There is a momentary sense of complete desolation and loneliness expressed either by striking or speaking. And then the parent comes to life again by showing love, for parental love is indestructible. This experience in one form or another may often be repeated, thus indicating the fundamental meaning of the death and resurrection of love in all of life. The child cannot win back his parent by reform, offering, self-punishment, or providing a scapegoat. The parent bridges the gap by the gift of healing love. This structure of human relationships provides a psychological background for understanding something of the meaning of the Cross and Resurrection in Christian doctrine.

Throughout all the years from nursery through primary grades, the child is asking, "Who am I?" "Who are you?" "How did we get here?" "Where are we going?" These are the basic problems of the Christian doctrine of man, and they need to be explained in relation to the child's experiences. The parents are the chief teachers, especially through providing in the home "a climate in which grace flourishes." As the child is accepted and loved and placed within a framework of dependable order, he is able to see his place in a limited world. Acceptance in the family is for him acceptance by God working through the family. Love from his parents when he is

most unlovable and demonic is the mediation of God's forgiveness and reconciliation. A home with both a moral and
a natural order gives him the sense of God's discipline and
judgment. And then he is able to indicate directions of growth
in both spiritual insight and character traits. He makes his
ethical decisions knowing that they represent something far
deeper than the whims of his parents, the mores of the community, or the rules of the school.

At the junior age, this becomes even more specific. One of
the best techniques here is the telling of a story in which
the children can anticipate the ethical decision that is required.
It must not be a thinly disguised exposure of their own specific
problems, but an imaginary story with a real ethical situation
that could realistically go either way. Raimundo de Ovies is a
past master of this, and in *The Church and the Children* his
story of the money in a boy's pocket (which belonged to his
mother) which would buy a ninety-eight cent air rifle is a
classic example of this approach. The boy had been sent to
the store for a cake of yeast, and he had ninety-eight cents
left, which his mother forgot to ask him for. At the sporting
goods store there was an air rifle in the window, which would
cost him ninety-eight cents with tax. He is tempted to buy it,
for he could hide it under his bed and use it without his
mother's knowledge. As the week goes by, his temptations
grow, and he almost buys the rifle. But at the last moment, he
decides that it was really his mother's money. About that time,
his mother remembers the change and asks him about it, and
he is so proud that he can return it to her. A few days later,
the boy has a birthday, and receives an air rifle. Such a story
needs no elaboration, and the boys and girls sit on the edge of
their seats sharing the boy's temptations and decisions with
him. Lying, cheating, and other problems may be approached
in much the same way. The same kind of approach may be
used with motivation, as in the graveyard story which Dean

de Ovies uses to show how a boy can do something if he really wants to.[6]

One of the most popular approaches has been through the so-called "A Child's Faith."

> "I believe in God above,
> I believe in Jesus' love,
> I believe his Spirit, too,
> Comes to teach me what to do.
> I believe that I can be
> True and loving, Lord, like thee." [7]

The first line is bad, because it points to a God in the sky which is objectionable on theological grounds. But the remainder of the creed speaks a child's language in terms of the example of Jesus and the power of the Spirit to help the child. Jesus as example is helpful in understanding the possibilities of Christian man at the junior age level. They are ready for a brief study of some aspects of the life of Jesus as these bear upon the problems they are facing. Here, our problem is understanding of the nature of man rather than Christian responsibility in ethical decisions, although the two are usually inseparable in any concrete situation. Further treatment of this subject in terms of individual and social ethics will be given in a later chapter.

Man's need of God, because man is a creature who tends to disobey God, is the major theme for the intermediate age level. For those about to be confirmed, there is this admonition: "Know this; that you are not able to do these things of yourself, nor to walk in the Commandments of God and to serve him, without his special grace; which you must learn at all times to call for by diligent prayer." This language is be-

---

[6] See *The Church and the Children*. New York: Morehouse-Gorham, pp. 120–126, 98–101.

[7] Quoted in *Prayers New and Old*. Cincinnati: Forward Movement, p. 11.

yond that of the average twelve year old, and even their psychology is pretty much set in seeking tasks equal to their
strength; but an analysis of their actual problems in their own
environments will convince them that they are actually in need
of the power of God.

Youth hymns often present this truth in ways which they
will appreciate. The second stanza of Edith Clayton's hymn
illustrates this:

> "Be with us, Lord; we kneel in supplication,
> In bonds of fellowship before thy throne;
> By fervent prayer, by willing consecration,
> Help us to know the Christ and make him known." [8]

Bates G. Burt has accomplished the same teaching with

> "O God of youth, whose Spirit in our hearts is stirring
> Hope and desire for noble lives and true,
> Keep us, we pray thee, steadfast and unerring;
> With light and love divine our souls endue." [9]

The prayer hymn of Richard of Chichester is equally effective:

> "Day by day,
> Dear Lord, of thee three things I pray:
> To see thee more clearly,
> Love thee more dearly,
> Follow thee more nearly,
> Day by day." [10]

On the high school level, a much more thorough approach
to the doctrine of man is possible. Using the eighth Psalm as
a starting point, the students look for the place of man in the
cosmos, as "but little lower than God." All *things* are in sub-

---

[8] *The Hymnal*, 1940. No. 509.
[9] *Ibid.*, No. 508.
[10] *Ibid.*, No. 429.

jection to man, except God and other men. They can see that there are two kinds of sin, the one of pride where man puts himself in place of God and seeks to control the destiny of his fellows, where goodness corrupts because it lacks any connection with the source of all goodness. This approach may be tied in with Jesus' condemnation of the righteous people of his own time, and especially of the prayer of the Pharisee who thanks God that he is not as other men. Without any prompting, some students will see these characteristics in their own congregation, sometimes in the minister, or elder, or warden, or sexton, or president of the women's group. Self-righteousness is a particularly unattractive form of sin. The Elder Son in the parable of the "Two Lost Sons" may be studied with profit.

Sin on the second level is the obvious type of sin of "the world, the flesh, and the devil." The unethical practices on any high school campus are the best illustrations, including cheating, lying, necking in excess, rebellion against parents, misuse of money, and various forms of delinquency. Men seem to fit the description by Shakespeare:

". . . but man, proud man!
Dress'd in a little brief authority,
Most ignorant of what he's most assured,
His glassy essence—like an angry ape,
Plays such fantastic tricks before high heaven,
As make the angels weep. . . ." [11]

The symbolism of the weeping of angels points to the sorrow and suffering of God, and this becomes the price of men's salvation.

The resources of the Christian Church are available to men with the sins and possibilities which we have described. Something can be done with repentance at every age level, but with

[11] *Measure for Measure*, Act II, Scene II.

high school students the terms may be defined and translated into their own experiences with richer meanings. They can begin to see that sin is "missing the mark," and that both individuals and society are "off the beam." They can tie this in with the narrow way and the broad highway that lead to heaven and hell respectively. They will understand what repentance means in terms of turning from one's sinful ways, or at least intending to turn, and doing what the Prodigal Son did when he "came to himself" and left the "far country" because he would rather be a "slave" in his father's household. Salvation is "deliverance from sinfulness" and is a gift of God through the Holy Spirit.

When the lost sheep jumps over a sheer cliff, he is completely separated from the God Shepherd. Sin is such a breaking of relationship with the Father. The loneliness of the sinner comes from being cut asunder from his better self, other men, and God. While the Shepherd's crook may sometimes keep the sheep from the edge of the cliff, once he has crashed on the rock below, no power of the sheep can bring him back to the flock. Just as Judas "went to his own place" so there is a place for unrepentant sinners. And yet God's love is great enough to seek for the lost sheep and bring him back to the fold. That is the glorious hope of the Gospel.

With this material translated into the experiences of high school pupils, it is necessary to see more deeply into the meaning of Christ and the grace of God. If the crucifixion actually changed man's relation to God, if Christ's death is a "pre-payment" for our sins, if God was in Christ for the purpose of establishing a new relationship with men, then the power of the Holy Spirit is available to help man do what he cannot do by himself. In the fellowship of the Church, these gifts of the Spirit are made available in worship and sacrament.

To put this truth in non-technical language and make it relevant to high school students is admittedly difficult. The

Christian faith is a religion of maturity, and no area of adolescence is even close to maturity. Abstractions are still impossible, but the middle adolescent is capable of faith, and by his
trust in God he may assimilate to himself the benefits which
God has bestowed upon him. "And if I . . . understand all
mysteries and all knowledge, and if I have all faith, so as to
remove mountains, but have not love, I am nothing" (I
Corinthians 13:2,A).

The gifts of God are available to all his creatures, at any age;
but just as the capacities change with the age-groups, so also
his gifts vary with the needs of these groups. The little child,
who is also a child of God, needs the blessings of God in a
different way from an adult. The Church provides Baptism
as a symbol of what God offers a child; it offers Confirmation
or the equivalent for the act of faith of which the adolescent
is capable and for the gifts of the Holy Spirit which are then
made available (although there is nothing mechanical or
magical about this); and it offers Holy Communion as the
permanent act of worship for mature Christians, with all the
powers of the living Christ being present for those who need
him.

The educational process must make God's creatures ready
for these gifts of grace which they so desperately need, but
it is in the personal relationship between God and his creatures
in the fellowship of his Church that these great relationships
are nurtured and grow. These gifts are part of the mystery of
God, and while they may be asked for, they may not be
coerced. We are God's creatures now, and it does not yet
appear what we shall be. We are heirs of God and joint-heirs
with Christ, and that is enough.

CHAPTER FIVE

THE FELLOWSHIP

EDUCATION is a social process, and the learner comes to his knowledge within one or another cell of society. For the purposes of Christian education, there are two organisms within society which may achieve the desired goals; one of these is the Christian family, and the other is the Church. From the beginning of their lives, children should feel and know that they are members of the Body of Christ, fully accepted within the Christian fellowship. If they are to be educated by and in the Church, they must feel free to take part in the Church's worship, where they are nurtured in the creative experience of being uniquely in the presence of God. It is only in this sense of belonging that children can come to a loyalty to the Church which is the fundamental social experience of being a Christian.

In order to understand the nature of the Church, attention must be given to its history. It is surprising how little attention is given to the development of the Church through the centuries, as if the Church began with the Reformation or with the arrival of the Pilgrim Fathers or with the construction of the new parish on the corner. Too often Church history begins with the Acts of the Apostles, skips to the Council of Nicaea, jumps to Martin Luther, and continues the story with the life of Livingstone. This may be satisfactory in the fifth grade, where the historical sense is only slightly developed; but it hardly gives an adult a sweeping view of the scope of the great tradition of the Christian community throughout the centuries.

While it is not the purpose of this chapter to review our knowledge of Church history, it is one of the most important subjects in the curriculum of the high school student. A developmental view of the Church is necessary for any understanding of the problems facing it today. It is important to realize that the creeds arose from controversies which rocked the whole of Christian civilization and were relevant to the times in which they arose. Every Christian should have some idea of how the ministry developed in the first few centuries, evolved into the complexities of the Roman system, and then was simplified by the changes at the time of the Reformation, with the resulting varieties in the non-Roman communions today. There are historical and theological reasons for all the theories of the ministry.

I

The Church is grounded in history. It finds its historic roots in Judaism, where the relationship between Yahweh and his people established God as Lord of history. Out of the mighty acts of God as recorded in the Bible came the covenants which issued in the life, death, and resurrection of Jesus Christ, and, with the coming of the Messiah, God entered a new covenantal relationship with the Jewish-Christian community. The Church is the people who have entered this covenant relationship, this agreement sealed by the death of Christ. The Church exists because God established it for the working out of his purposes, and this is the theological justification of the Church's existence.

"The Church's one foundation is Jesus Christ her Lord." The term, Body of Christ, signifies that what God began in

Christ is extended in history by the organism, the fellowship, the community, which is rooted and grounded in Christ. It is not the function of the Church to duplicate any other organism in society, but to do its own work. This is the sense in which the slogan, "Let the Church be the Church," has significance. The Church is primarily a worshiping society, provided by the grace of God with a ministry of the Word and Sacraments, to lead men into complete commitment to the God of Jesus Christ. It is a Christian fellowship, and within the community there is the possibility of the greatest demonstration of Christian love. It is this quality of life within the fellowship which commends the Church to the world, and in so far as the members of the Church fail in this purpose the world condemns it. Yet the most important justification of the Church's life is not the perfection of its members so much as the ability of the corporate life of the Church to point beyond itself to God. It is the function of the Church to provide instruction and leadership in Christian truth and living, not only by its preaching but also in its entire educational program. Reaching out from the Church, and yet including all its members, is the ideal of the Good Samaritan as extended to all aspects of a full and rich pastoral ministry. In so far as the Church is alive, it never is satisfied with giving the message to its own people. There is an outreaching which extends to the whole world and which underlies the missionary motive; without missions, the Church dies. Finally, as an organization, the Church is never limited to national barriers, for in its ideal form it is always universal and in practice it has been remarkably successful in crossing the barriers set up by economics and war. The Church, then, is a worshiping society, in which may be found Christian fellowship, instruction in Christian truth and living, genuine pastoral concern, missionary hopes, and supranational influence and fellowship.[1]

[1] See my *What We Can Believe*, pp. 102–123.

"The visible Church of Christ is a congregation of faithful men, in which the pure Word of God is preached, and the Sacraments be duly administered according to Christ's ordinance, in all those things that of necessity are requisite to the same." [2] This simple definition is acceptable to most Christians, but there is difference of opinion as to what constitutes valid preaching and sacraments. Our concern is not to define a denomination, however, but to point to the fundamental functions of a Christian Church and what we believe is involved in all groups which qualify as Christian.

The preaching of the Word involves two important elements. The first is that preaching should find its source in the Christian revelation, for it is the Gospel of Christ which is being offered to the congregation. When we come to the problem of authority, we will see how the Scriptures are involved in all teaching and preaching; but at this point it needs only to be indicated that the chief source for all preaching of the Word is Holy Scripture. The second observation is that because the Word of God is relevant to all of life, the concern of the Church's preaching message can never be limited to any so-called spiritual aspect of life. All of life is the creation of God, and thus the Gospel is relevant to every human experience.

The two sacraments ordained by Christ are integral parts of the Church's life. They are signs of grace by which God works in men to strengthen them and to make their faith more effective.

Baptism is a sign of spiritual cleansing, of death to one's sin, of new birth in obedience to God. This is symbolized by the use of water, wherein the person is baptized in the Name of the Father, and of the Son, and of the Holy Ghost. With this form, any Baptism by a lay person is normally accepted by

[2] 13th Article of Religion, Methodist Church. 19th Article, Episcopal Church.

most denominations, except where immersion of adults is the only tradition. For a valid adult Baptism, the person to be baptized must declare his repentance and acknowledge his faith in Jesus Christ as Lord and Savior. Baptism is not only a badge of being a Christian, but is the act by which men are grafted into the Body of Christ and become members of the family of God. It is incorporation into the fellowship of all believers. It sets in motion those forces by which the grace of God assists men in getting free from the influences which predispose them to sin. It does not stop sin, but it introduces new factors into the environment and into the person which make it easier to reject temptations.

Where Baptism of infants is common, an opportunity is always provided to renew the baptismal vows at the age of discretion. Infant Baptism is not contrary to the interpretation given above, for the sponsors provide the faith which a child cannot give, and the Church receives them so that they may receive God's grace and grow up in the household of faith. The illustration is frequently used of birth, citizenship, and infant baptism: A child is born into a human family without his consent; he is born a citizen of a country by the same act; he is made a Christian, and is born in the family of God, by the new birth of Baptism. The reception of the child is by family, country, and Church; the act of faith in each case is provided by someone who is concerned for his welfare. When he reaches the age of discretion, he takes responsibility for the family in which he is born, he accepts the right to vote in the country of which he is a citizen, and he renews his vows as a Christian and selects the particular denomination through which he will express that loyalty. In the meantime, he has received all the heritage of family, country, and Church to which he is rightfully entitled.

It is interesting to note that where Baptism is postponed to a later age, a new service of "dedication" of infants is increasing in popularity to meet the need of making the infant "a member of Christ, the child of God, and an inheritor of the kingdom of heaven." The experience of the ancient Church in using Baptism and confirmation as separated portions of the same rite is being vindicated by those who in their own way are returning to this practice as well as by those who have kept it. Confirmation is not to be considered a "sacrament of the Gospel," but it is the completion of Baptism on the part of the believer, and becomes a channel for the strengthening gifts of the Holy Spirit.

The second major sacrament is open to more controversy than Baptism. The controversies that have surrounded the Lord's Supper have made it one of the divisive elements of Christendom rather than the "sacrament of unity." It has become associated with the arguments about a valid ministry; it has been interpreted in terms of closed membership; and it has in some cases been dreadfully neglected by those who have preferred to emphasize other aspects of the life of the Christian community. More hard thinking and re-thinking is necessary here than in almost any other area of theology.

For sound teaching in sacramental worship, we need a clear idea of basic meanings of the Holy Communion. It is thought of among various Christian groups as sacrifice, communion, eucharist, Lord's Supper, and "breaking of bread." It has significance for today's worshipers under all of these headings.

One of the most primitive forms of worship is sacrifice. The sacrifice of human beings, goats, and other animals to a hungry God is common among most early religious practices. It is found in this form among the Israelites in the Old Testament. But very early in the experience of the Hebrews, sacrificial worship began to take on more rich and deep meanings. Always a sacrifice was a gift of something worthful in itself, and it came to symbolize the gift of the self. It was because Abraham was willing to give God anything he asked for that

Isaac was offered. A sacrifice, moreover, was always a cult practice, and it came to have significance as an expression of fellowship; it was ceremonial in the best sense of that word —a giving of what was worthful to God by an individual who was also part of a people who believed that God desired and accepted such gifts. It is true that ceremonial often degenerated into priestcraft and substituted for good works, but usually this occurred in the cults opposed to Yahwism, as in the story of Bel and the Dragon. Bel is an idol who eats the food offered to it. Daniel, as a worshiper of Yahweh, claims the idol cannot eat food, and by his detective work he proves to the king that the priests and their wives and children have a trap door under the altar through which they come and eat the food when the temple is locked. This story is found in the Apocrypha in some Bibles.

Almost always, a sacrifice was offered against the background of the conviction of sin, sometimes as appeasement of an angry God but often as a symbol of a desire for forgiveness. There is propitiation, in that God becomes favorable to man through a sacrificial act. A sacrifice is also used for a sealing of a covenant, and thus it is a sign that man accepts the agreement that God has offered him. Finally, man's sacrifice is thought of against the background of the one sufficient sacrifice of the Cross. Any thing that man can offer is simply too finite and limited to account for the tremendous horror of man's sin. So all Christians alike, no matter how they differ in their interpretation of the sacrament of the Lord's Supper, are in agreement at this one point: they see in Christ's self-offering an opening of a way of salvation, once and for all, that men may offer a sacrificial devotion to one who loved the world so much that he sacrificed his own Son to save that world.

All worship in this sense is a sacrifice, a self-giving of the worshiper to Almighty God. We are already God's, and thus anything that we offer him is already his. The form of homage due the Creator by the creature is an offering of the self, both soul and body, as a "reasonable, holy, and living sacrifice." This is accomplished not by the individual, however much he may feel the desire, but by him as a member of the cultus; for the social and corporate nature of sacramental worship is basic; it is a formal and ritual act of the fellowship.

Different points of view are to be expected at this point. Some individuals and some groups will prefer to emphasize the idea of sacrifice as a gift, others as a pledge of fellowship, or as a formal acceptance of an agreement, or as the prelude to God's forgiveness.[3] Protestants insist that the one, sufficient sacrifice of Christ is never repeated, and that the sacrifice in the Holy Communion is of prayer and praise and humble heart.

The various terms applied to the Lord's Supper emphasize one or another side of the truth. The Eucharist means simply thanksgiving and refers originally to the fact that Jesus gave thanks before the breaking of the bread at the Last Supper, and it is a particularly fitting term to describe our offering of thanks at the Holy Table. Communion refers to the "real presence" of Christ and that the receivers of the bread and wine are in communion with Christ, and also that there is fellowship among the "communion of all faithful people." The Lord's Supper indicates that we are eating in the Lord's presence. The original term, "breaking of bread," comes from the story of the Last Supper and puts the emphasis on fellowship.

The definition of a sacrament accepted by many Christian groups is admirably summarized in the Episcopal Church's "Offices of Instruction": "an outward and visible sign of an inward and spiritual grace given unto us; ordained by Christ himself, as a means whereby we receive this grace, and a pledge to assure us thereof. . . . The Sacrament of the Lord's Supper

[3] Cf. *Doctrine in the Church of England*, p. 155.

was ordained for the continual remembrance of the sacrifice
of the death of Christ, and of the benefits which we receive
thereby. . . . The benefits . . . are the strengthening and refreshing of our souls." [4]

Some will ask, "How is Christ present?" To this question
there has never been a satisfactory answer. The Roman Church
has said that the elements actually become in substance the
Body and Blood of Christ, and this doctrine of "transubstantia-
tion" was repudiated at the time of the Reformation by the
Protestant Churches. Lutherans presented the idea of "con-
substantiation," in which Christ is present *with* the bread and
wine. Anglicans were satisfied to talk about the "real presence,"
and it has been defined in various ways: one of these approaches the Lutheran doctrine of Christ being present "under
the forms of bread and wine"; another goes toward the other
extreme of saying Christ is present in the hearts of those who
truly believe; and a third view says that a change takes place
in spiritual power but not in substance. The important thing
is that Christ is present in such a way that there is communion with him and power is received. There are some
groups who would not be interested in these problems and
would say simply that the Lord's Supper is a memorial meal.
All groups are agreed that the means whereby Christ is received
is faith.

One other problem comes to the fore in understanding the
sacrament of the Lord's Supper. The sacramental principle is
involved with the meaning of the priesthood. For Roman
Catholics, a sacrificing priesthood is essential to the sacrifice
of the "Mass." For many other groups, a ministry recognized
as valid must perform the sacrament. Because the churches
have not come to common understanding on the nature of
the ministry, they are kept apart in the fellowship of the Lord's
Supper. The major interpretations are those of Congrega-

[4] *Book of Common Prayer*, pp. 292–293.

tionalists, with office conferred by the local congregation, Lutheran, with a priesthood of all believers and ordinands representing them, Calvinist, with ordination by presbyters acting in their episcopal capacity, and Anglican, with ordination by bishops in historic succession. Except in the United Church of South India, these forms of polity have been unable to achieve union, and because the Lord's Supper depends upon the ministry, there is no way to complete fellowship at the Lord's Table across these lines.

The Church quite clearly is not any one denomination; it is the "Body of Christ," of which all baptized people are members. The creeds describe the Church as one, holy, catholic, and apostolic, meaning that it is one in its loyalty to Christ, holy in that it is the agent of the Holy Spirit, catholic in that it is universal in its scope, and apostolic because it derives its basic teachings from the apostles' times. It is in this sense that we believe in the one, holy, catholic Church. The trouble with the Church is, as Bishop Parsons says, it "has never been Catholic enough." [5]

The Church is organized to meet the needs of its members. There is no crisis of life which is not covered by the work and worship of the Church. There are services of baptism, confirmation, marriage, visitation of the sick, burial. Being born, growing up, getting married, being sick, dying—all are related to the Gospel of Jesus Christ by the life of the congregation in its prayers and concern for its members.

The way to become a Christian is to enter the Church. It is possible to be a good man and even to accept the ideals for which Jesus stood without being a Christian. The Christian is one who follows Christ as Lord and Savior, worships God in his Church, and works and prays and gives for the extension of Christ's kingdom on earth.

[5] In R. C. Miller and H. H. Shires, eds., *Christianity and the Contemporary Scene*. New York: Morehouse-Gorham, p. 114.

II

The relevance of the nature and function of the Church to every child committed to its care should be obvious. If every baptized person is a member of the Church, the fundamental principle of every congregation should be the granting of these rights of "belongingness" to every child. The Church's preparation for receiving the child begins with the education of his parents, making clear to them their place in the life of the Church and their responsibility for the Christian nurture of their child. More and more, birth and Baptism are accompanied by educational guidance of the parents, and many of the clergy will not baptize a child until the parents and godparents have received instruction. This is followed by the cradle roll instruction, so that the child is treated as a member of the Church before he is old enough for nursery class.

Baptism is the child's initiation into the Church. It is an instrument of God's act and also a symbol of what God intends. The agents of the Church include the godparents, parents, and congregation. The *parents are the Church* to the infant, teaching not by word but by relationship that God is dependable and loving, and that God wills us to belong to him. In some Church schools, the nursery child is brought into the Church proper (nave, sanctuary) for a brief appearance, perhaps for an opening hymn with a junior choir procession and for the Lord's Prayer, which he has learned for the corporate experience of worship and not because he understands any of it. Thus he belongs to a worshiping congregation in the actual Church building. Then he goes to his class, where he may play with blocks, enjoying his manipulations, and feeling secure. He plays with other three year olds who also feel secure in their own room; but they belong to the whole Church as well as to the nursery room. As friendships develop, he might be led to say, "We have fun at *my* Church. Thank you, God, for my Church." The pastor should visit the class occasionally, often enough so that the children will associate him with the brief leadership of their worship in the Church. It will help a great deal if his parents are sufficiently interested to know what is going on in the nursery class and will correlate his Sunday and weekday activities, and perhaps will also attend Church with him. The importance of this age for the development of loyalty to the Church cannot be overemphasized, for long before the child knows any theology or any Bible he is building the patterns of his personality and his habits of loyalty. This is the time to begin following the slogan, "Put habit on the side of religion."

The time for an extensive investigation of the functions of the Church comes at about the third grade, age eight. Except for the fact that Jesus Christ founded the Church, there is no room for history. The emphasis should be primarily on the functioning of the local congregation. With plenty of activities planned, there should be complete satisfaction of the children's curiosity about the Church buildings; they should see and hear everything, tour everywhere, and have all their questions answered. They might construct a model Church. And always they should be reminded in creative ways that this Church is theirs and that they are members. Opportunity should be offered for them to observe a baptism of infants, children, and adults; and where public baptism is customary this can be done quite regularly at the morning service of "junior Church." They should see a wedding in the Church. They should visit an adult service, with proper preparation in advance; and then they should proceed to study the outline and nature of the adult service they visited and compare it with their "junior Church." If the psychology of worship is sound, they will discover enough similarities between the services to feel at home in both. They might work up their own service of worship, rehearse it, conduct it, and evaluate it. In all of these ways, they are coming to an understanding of the functions of the Church and of their part in it.

With confirmation customary at the age of twelve, the preceding year or sixth grade course should return to the subject of worship in some detail. Study of the hymnal and manuals of worship may be worked out in terms of sixth grade experiences and the anticipation of confirmation. The Bible as a source of worship offers a fruitful means of approach. The meaning of covenants, basic to an understanding of the nature of the Church, might be approached in terms of the experience of gangs, with their various kinds of rules and loyalty according to law, heart, and sealing of agreements with blood. Little can be done about the Lord's Supper until it is part of the boy's or girl's experience.

A fruitful approach to the place of the sermon is suggested in Mary White's *New Testament and You* for seventh or eighth grade. The unit begins with the question, "What Makes a Sermon Good?" This works back to the New Testament source, which is the letter of James, and at the conclusion of examining some of the startling illustrations in this magnificent homiletical treatment, the unit is brought to its conclusion with "the sermon *I* would preach."

Dora Chaplin shows how this approach is combined remarkably with the meaning of the Church for seventh graders in a sermon actually prepared and given to a congregation of adults and children:

"In the ninth verse of the thirteenth Chapter of the Gospel according to St. Matthew, Jesus said: 'Who hath ears to hear, let him hear.'

"If a newspaper reporter should stop you on your way out of Church today and ask you what you got out of the service, and you told the truth, what would you say?

"Would you have to admit that you had come here to pass

the time—if the weather was bad—or just to talk to the neighbors? If you were asked what the lessons were about, would you know? And did you pray, or while the minister was saying prayers for you, did your thoughts wander?

"Suppose the reporter asked about your children. Would you have to plead guilty of bribing your children to come to Church, to frightening them by saying they'd not get into Heaven unless they came to Church, or to forcing them to go without any idea of what Church is for? It is hard to make a child believe in God if his parent does not. It is hard for a boy or girl to know what is expected of him in Church if he is not told something beforehand at home. He will realize he comes here not to fool, but to worship—if you do. And he can understand what God is like if you say only that you come to Church to confess your sins and that if you do God will help you—that He isn't angry, but you should not sin any more.

"God is the Reporter, asking you that question today. He is here, in and outside of Church, on Sunday and all the rest of the week, asking you not what you got out of Church, but what you put in." [6]

Another great source at this age is the hymnal. "The Church's One Foundation," "The Church of God Is Stablished," "Oh Where Are Kings and Empires Now?" "We Love the Place, O God," and many others are easily interpreted by twelve year olds.

For the high school age, the challenge of the Church to them might well be the central theme. If they feel that they belong to the congregation, it is possible to build their loyalty to the universal Church of God. The theme is set by the third stanza of William P. Merrill's great hymn:

"Rise up, O men of God!
The Church for you doth wait:

[6] Dora P. Chaplin, *Children and Religion.* New York: Scribners, pp. 89–90.

Her strength unequal to her task;
Rise up, and make her great!" [7]

They are aware of the weaknesses of organized Christianity, and they would like the prayer of Archbishop Laud:

"O gracious Father, we humbly beseech thee for thy Holy Catholic Church; that thou wouldst be pleased to fill it with all truth, in all peace. Where it is corrupt, purify it; where it is in error, direct it; where in any thing it is amiss, reform it. Where it is right, establish it; where it is in want, provide for it; where it is divided, reunite it; for the sake of him who died and rose again, and ever liveth to make intercession for us, Jesus Christ, thy Son, our Lord. *Amen.*" [8]

The attempt to illustrate the fundamental educational philosophy of this book was worked out in a course for high school students, entitled *The Challenge of the Church.*[9] The beginning challenge was "The Church and the Crises of Life," which indicated how the Church was ready to help in every crisis and in every kind of trouble. After a brief review of Church history, there was a unit of six sessions on "The Church's Faith." Three sessions deal with "Prayer and Worship" and then the course turns to denominational effectiveness on the national level, with a project involving correspondence with national headquarters. The horizon continues to widen with four sessions on the ecumenical movement under the title, "How Wide Is the Church?" Then the course turns back on itself and examines the responsibilities of these particular high school students to the Church with "How Do We Live with the Church?" and this leads finally to the problem, "What, Then, Is the Church?" with a final decision for the Church worked out in terms of their own service of worship.

[7] *Hymnal,* 1940. No. 535.
[8] *Book of Common Prayer,* p. 37.
[9] New York: Morehouse-Gorham.

Other aspects of the Church's nature and work need to be taught. Church history is necessary if we are to understand the work of God as Lord of history. Until the fourth grade, however, practically no history is possible except for isolated stories relating to current experiences. Bible history becomes a possibility with the fourth or fifth grade, but without much theological interpretation. Biography and the appeal to hero-worship is almost always the best approach.

It is with the ninth grade that we can begin to work at the problems posed by the history of the Church. One of the best examples of this is Mary Jenness' *Climbers of the Steep Ascent*,[10] which is remarkable for its ability to relate historical situations to the life experience of intermediates and to capture their imaginations with vivid and accurate stories about twenty of the greatest men who were also centers of strategic movements within the Church. When supplemented by Roland Bainton's *Church of Our Fathers*[11] and Sara Abbott's *Story of the Christian Church*,[12] with the latter at the senior high school level, much fine material is available which is well related to the interests and capacities of this period.

The world-wide mission of the Church may be used as soon as there is any geographical imagination on the part of the child. A good unit on missions appears in some series as early as the first grade, and fourth and fifth grade boys and girls are able to follow maps without too great trouble.

The best approach to the Church's worship is through participation.[13] Here is creative and life-centered education at its best, if it is at all relevant. The experiences of worship in "junior Church" should lead automatically to a feeling of at-

[10] New York: Morehouse-Gorham.
[11] New York: Scribners.
[12] Boston: Pilgrim Press.
[13] See my *Guide for Church School Teachers*. Chicago: Wilcox & Follett (Cloister Press), pp. 59–70.

homeness in adult worship. The big transition in many denominations comes with confirmation and the first Communion. Here is the opportunity to teach the boys and girls the meaning of the Lord's Supper historically and in terms of its modern significance. The corporateness of this great act is something they will feel as they partake in full equality with the rest of the congregation of the presence of the living Christ. They may be disappointed if they are led to expect too much emotional reaction, and they need to learn that it is the regular participation in Holy Communion that leads to the fulfillment of the promise of the strengthening powers of the Holy Spirit. It is not easy to explain the mystery of the presence of the living Christ to any age-group, but within the congregation of faithful communicants it is possible for them to share the mystery and its meaning for them. Before the time of confirmation, the average child will see nothing but inexplicable activity in Holy Communion, so that its educational value is primarily in terms of pageantry, although some congregations have claimed to have success, educationally speaking, with a children's communion as part of the Church school worship.

Several story books of children exploring various aspects of the Church's life have been quite successful. Some have taken an imaginary family through various experiences within the local congregation and others have taken them on field trips to New York and national headquarters. A little of this may prove quite an aid at several age-levels.

The most important thing, as far as understanding the Church is concerned, is the right start. The pleasant feeling of loyalty to an institution, beginning at the earliest age with security in the Church's nursery, and leading on to an exploration of the local Church at the primary age, sets the stage for all subsequent steps. As the horizons expand, so should the loyalties, so that in time loyalty to the local Church will become loyalty to the denomination, and to the ecumenical movement, culminating in a sense of loyalty to the entire Body of Christ, which is the Holy Catholic Church in which we believe when we say the creeds. But never must the wider loyalty undermine the sense of responsibility to the local Church, for one can never belong to *the* Church without being an active member of *a* congregation. At the high school level, and in a simpler way at the time of confirmation, the students should come to grips with their duties and how they can be fulfilled in detail at their age. How can they help make the fellowship of the local and larger Church more fully Christian? What specific work can they do as Church members? How can they learn? How much should they give, in terms of both the local congregation and of the world-wide mission of the Church? The answers to these questions will depend on how well the youth of the Church have been integrated into the total educational program and life of the congregation, for there is no use in discussing impossible and improbable projects when these young people have no authority.

Finally, the question about the Church is not ultimately, "What can the Church do for me?" but "What can I do for the Church?" The first question is always relevant, and there is much that the Church does for every member that would not otherwise be done, for the Church is the divinely appointed channel of God's grace. The second question is the ultimate one, however, for the disciple is both a learner and a follower, and as a follower of Christ he is one who is willing to lose his life in the service of his fellow men.

If we are to think of the Church in its highly exalted terms as the Body of Christ or the extension of the Incarnation or as God's agent of redemption, we must look beyond what it is to what God intended it to be—a congregation of faithful people, in a covenant relation with God, in which God's Word is truly preached, and through the sacramental life of which God's grace is truly channeled. Faithful people may not always be good in the eyes of the world, but what is important about them is that their faith is pointing in the right direction.

CHAPTER SIX
GRACE

O NE of the great words of the Christian heritage is "Grace." Here is the telling of God's favor toward man, of God's kindness and mercy, of God's free gift of himself to his creatures which provides power for men to overcome their sins, of God's forgiveness and re-establishment of the right relation between himself and sinful men. Through faith and through the sacraments, this grace is bestowed on men.

Grace, then, is God-in-action, as he makes use of personal relationships to forgive and strengthen his creatures. It includes the gifts of the Holy Spirit. God is gracious, kind, merciful, good-willed, and shows his favor to men. It is often mediated through other men, and to children through their parents.

The doctrine of grace is prominent in all theologies, and the great theologians of Catholic and Protestant heritage have equally emphasized its importance. Yet, strangely enough, there is little teaching about the experience of God's grace in most Church school courses, either in terms of sacramental worship or of power for living. With all the need for faith, with all the limitations of men which can be overcome only by the grace of God, there are, in most Church school materials, assumptions that if only the pupils learn enough they can be good Christians. It is the old heresy of Pelagius, writ large; it has been disproved by the experiences of Christians throughout the ages, and yet the influence of modern optimism about the essential goodness of man has brought it to the forefront of educational philosophy. The creature being taught in our Church schools needs to know and experience the grace of God, and he will be strengthened and refreshed when he learns to place his hope and trust in God.

I

The dominant view of grace in the Bible is that of Paul. It is not the only Christian interpretation, but it has been the common one during the history of the Church. We shall deal first with Paul's presentation and then decide how it should be altered for our purposes. We need to remember that Paul's theology stems directly from his conversion, and his doctrine of grace tended to justify and elaborate his vital conversion experience. His thought was conditioned by careful training in the ways of the Hebrew religion and in the rough-hewn idea of grace in the Old Testament, in which grace was to find favor with Yahweh or with a superior. Certainly Paul's favor in the sight of his Risen Lord was neither merited nor asked for; his status as a new creature was an outright gift, which he could not resist.[1]

For Paul, grace was tied in closely with what God knew beforehand about men's behavior. God is arbitrary in whom he chooses, "for it is God which worketh in you both to will and to do of his good pleasure" (Phil. 2:13,KJ), but Paul never loses sight of the other side of the paradox as he says, "I do not frustrate the grace of God" (Gal. 2:21,KJ). Therefore, grace is the product of God's election and man's free acceptance at the same time.

[1] See N. P. Williams, *The Grace of God*; Leonard Hodgson, *The Grace of God in Faith and Philosophy*; Reinhold Niebuhr, *The Nature and Destiny of Man*, II.

Grace is the means of justification. We are justified, or made upright by faith in Jesus Christ, through giving ourselves to him, and it is the redemption made possible by the work of Christ that gives us grace. Our access to grace is by faith, and nothing else. "Therefore," writes Paul, "since we are justified by faith, we have peace with God through our Lord Jesus Christ. Through him we have obtained access to this grace in which we stand, and we rejoice in our hope of sharing the glory of God" (Rom. 5:1–2,A). We can do nothing to merit this favor from God. Grace is always something more than we deserve, thus putting the emphasis on God's loving good will rather than upon his justice.

This interpretation of grace is illustrated in Paul's attitude toward the law. Paul is skeptical of any works of merit. He says we do not live under the law. "For by grace you have been saved through faith," says the author of Ephesians, "and this is not your own doing, it is the gift of God—not because of works, lest any man should boast" (Eph. 2:8–9,A). This is the kind of thinking which led Augustine to say, "Love God and do as you please," but Paul kept a balance by bringing in the moral law, as distinct from the ceremonial and ritual laws of the Old Testament. There was a moral fibre in the backbone of Paul's idea of grace which at the same time opposed a cold legalism and kept God's creatures moral. The God of grace is still the God of the prophets.

It is possible to fall from grace, and this leaves an unresolved paradox. How could anyone fall from irresistible grace, except by foreknowledge, thus invalidating God's own election? Only thus can Paul make room for freedom and moral responsibility. If grace is persuasive and influential rather than irresistible, there is a solution to the dilemma in which Paul finds himself; and in other portions of his writings he indicates that he would so interpret it. Man is free to "fall from grace" and in Acts we read that Paul and Barnabas "urged them to continue in the grace of God" (Acts 13:43,A).

Grace is also associated with a divine calling or vocation. "Our talents differ with the grace that is given us" (Rom. 12:6,M). "By the grace of God, I am what I am" (I Cor. 15:10,KJ). Here we have grace used in the sense of a commission, wherewith God calls us and sends us and provides the means for doing God's work, for "God is able to give you all grace in full measure; so that ever having enough of all things, you may be full of every good work" (II Cor. 9:8,B).

Grace is basically a source of power. Grace is not a way to escape pain and travail, but a means for transcending them. Grace as power is inescapably associated with the Cross of Christ, so that any suffering now present is not comparable to the glory which is God's gift. It is God who lifts us from the depths of our own misery and sin and sufferings and raises us to the heights. Grace may be the power to achieve specific daily tasks which normally we could not do. The spiritual gifts, with all their diversities, are from the same Spirit and the same grace. Grace brings power out of weakness.

The power of God's grace does not eliminate the possibility of further evil and sin. For no possibility of good can ever be divorced from the inclination toward sin. Thus grace always involves forgiveness, and before forgiveness there comes judgment. The relation between the words, "give" and "forgive," is close enough to suggest that there was a connection in experience as well as in language. There was the practice of forgiveness in the early Church, following the example of Christ, and this was in turn ascribed to the "gracious" nature of God in Christ.

It was not long before Paul's opening formula for his letters was expanded from "Grace and peace to you," to "Grace, mercy, and peace." This change indicated the richness of the meaning of grace, and mercy was not something added to it, but the emphasis on mercy, the association of grace with baptism, pointing to moral goodness as the test and outcome, and the relation of grace to immortality are indicative of the ever-widening meaning of the center of Pauline theology, which was no longer Paul's but which belonged to the whole Church.[2]

Now grace may be so widely interpreted that it covers "God-in-action," and this tendency may be seen in the history of theology, when God does everything and man can do nothing without grace. This is true to the experience that man is absolutely dependent upon God, but it leaves nothing for man to do. The view in the Synoptic Gospels is much simpler than this. Jesus seems to say that man has real freedom to turn to God, and when this happens God acts to save him from the depths of hell.

Horace Bushnell pointed out that while the greatest saints admitted their dependence upon God, they never hesitated to affirm their integrity before God. A man with integrity is spiritually whole before other men and God. He is a genuinely "whole-intent" man. There are some "pretendedly orthodox Christians" who rely on unmerited grace, and "ten times a day they declare that they will know nothing, but Christ and him crucified, and lest they should miss such a faith, they do not spare to crucify him abundantly themselves." [3]

A religion of grace begins with man's part, which is wholeness of intent as preparation for the redeeming efficacy of grace. "As certainly then as I come into right intent, I shall come into faith, and trust myself to him, as a means of becoming what I have undertaken to become." [4] Grace is not superseded, but the universality of God's grace is affirmed as a

---

[2] See James Moffatt, *Grace in the New Testament*. New York: Harpers, pp. 102, 136, 299–301, 312–313.

[3] Bushnell, *Christ and His Salvation*, p. 188. The entire essay on "Integrity and Grace" is to the point.

[4] *Ibid.*, p. 190.

dependable factor in Christian experience. It denies the rigidity of the doctrine of election without contradicting God's sovereignty. It asserts the universal truth that Jesus Christ "by the grace of God should taste death for every man" (Hebrews 2:9,KJ).

This leads us to another point, implied certainly in the Synoptic tradition and made explicit in the writings of John Oman, that God's grace is persuasive rather than irresistible. The analogy of the difference between conscription and volunteering for war service gives us insight into God's working among men. God challenges us with an overwhelming sense of duty, which we may accept or reject. He uses his persuasive grace to call us to a task so compelling, so daring, so high, that we volunteer to enter his service; and then he gives us the power, if we will accept it, which enables us to do his will.

This places the gift of grace on a new level. It is not a question of stimulus and response, and there is nothing impersonal about it. It is a gracious personal relationship which is uplifting and power-giving within the organic framework of the Creator-creature and creature-creature societies. When grace is irresistible it cannot be gracious! "Grace," says Oman, "has always a convex side towards God, and a concave side towards man. Taken separately, they are contradictory and opposite, but, united, they are as perfectly one as the convex and concave sides of one line. As acts of grace and acts of will, they are sheer conflicting forces; in the gracious relation to us of the Father of our spirits, their harmony is the essential expression of our fellowship. Yet, the harmony of love, not of absorption, of personal agreement, not of pantheistic oneness, can be won only as we realize the contradiction and see how God overcomes it, by accepting it." God's grace saves our freedom, and therefore is both moral and religious. But it requires integrity rather than morality, for "grace is precisely grace because, *though wholly concerned with moral goodness, it does not at all depend on how moral we are."* [5]

When we have the strength and courage to overcome the obstacles which face us, this power is the gift of God, even though we may interpret it in terms of latent energies, glandular reaction, or the result of prayer. When we have the patience and comfort of accepting what is inevitable, without distortion of our visions or our honest hopes, that, too, is the gift of God. And the ability to determine which should be overcome and which should be accepted is the most important factor of all, for it is this insight into possibilities as distinguished from dreams which is the gift of God's Spirit to every man who will keep himself sensitive, aware, and curious, using every power of discernment to exhaust the alternatives and then making his final decision in full trust in the living and gracious Father. We may believe that "with God all things are possible" and "that all things work together for good for them that love God," and at the same time recognize that all things are not possible for us in the providence of God.[6]

The significance of this doctrine of grace is abundantly illustrated by a casual accumulation of statistics from John Suter's *Book of English Collects*. While there are forty-three prayers which refer to faith, there are seventy-three which refer to grace. The various aspects of God's gifts of grace are mentioned, including justification, falling from grace, freedom, power, strength, help, protection, healing, freedom from fear, forgiveness, wisdom. A remarkable summary is found in this prayer:

> "Give them grace, we pray thee, to stand fast in the faith, to obey thy Word, and to abide in thy love; that,

[5] John Oman, *Grace and Personality*. Cambridge: at the University Press, pp. 86, 188–189, 194. Oman's italics.
[6] See my *What We Can Believe*, pp. 188–189.

being made strong by thy Holy Spirit, they may resist temptation and overcome evil, and may rejoice in the life that now is, and dwell with thee in the life that is to come." [7]

II

As we turn to the educational application of the doctrine of grace, it is obvious that little has been done to build this great experience into the lives of children. While the experience of God's grace is present, it is never clearly perceived or explained in terms of God's free gift of power and favor and forgiveness. In various vocabularies, children express what God's grace means to them, and they find it in their environment and in the interaction between persons rather than as direct access to God through faith.

We can begin to see what very small children experience when they make their own "Thank you, God" prayers. At the top of the list come food, Mother's loving care, brothers and sisters, friends, animals, happy hours at Church school, sleep, and other simple needs. There is nothing abstract about these experiences, but they are part of the environment and activities of the children which may be ascribed to the grace of God. They do not formulate the kind of abstract ideas which are descriptive of some of their fundamental needs, such as the sense of security and stability.

With the very youngest, the relationship between God and even these gifts of his grace are not clearly seen. While the little child has not developed a sense of cause and effect, he may find it incongruous to thank God for the turkey that he saw Daddy buy. He is more aware of his Mother's love than of God's relationship to her love. Yet, in order to make the child aware of God's gracious gifts, no custom is more im-

[7] J. W. Suter, *Book of English Collects*. New York: Harpers, No. 397.

portant than grace at meals, for this is a family expression of dependence upon God rather than simply a thanking God for food.

With primary children, there are many simple illustrations of the need of God's grace. It may appear in their prayers, as in "Dear God, make Mommy well," or "Help me, God, to be a better boy," or "Forgive me, Lord, for telling that lie." In such simple expressions as these is found the need for the help which God gives in healing, strengthening, and forgiving. They may begin to see how God upholds them in all that they do, although usually their experience is limited to specific needs on particular occasions.

This experience is widened as the children become older. The juniors will think of the closeness of God when they are in various situations, as when they are alone or when they are sad, or when they are making friends, whether they are at Church, or school, or playground, and at night. One prayer by a group of eleven year olds concludes: "Without thee there would be no world."

Often children of junior age will think of God as an unseen helper. Sometimes a boy will say that God helps him with his school lessons, and when he is queried, he will say, "God won't do my lessons for me, but if I think of God he keeps me at my work until it is done." [8] These boys and girls think of God as a helpful spirit of power, and he helps them chiefly to be good. A frank discussion of this relation to God in a class of fifth or sixth graders can be illuminating. The pupils will begin to see the source of strength in the heroes of the Church against the background of the help God gives them to do what they ought in their relations with their fellows, in their studies, and when they face difficulties. The related subjects of faith and prayer, which will be discussed in detail in later

[8] See Mildred and Frank Eakin, *Your Child's Religion*. New York: Macmillan, p. 6.

chapters, are involved here, of course, for we have already shown the relation of faith to grace.

If God is working for good through us, by the free gift of his grace, the children of this age will always ask, "Why are some people bad?" This throws us back to the nature of man as a creature as discussed in chapter Four. Perhaps the best approach may be through an understanding of family life, where the parents use every influence to encourage good actions. They provide motives for obedience, for loyalty, for honesty, and for other virtues, and yet children do not always use their power to do what they ought to do. They know they should practice on the violin, or help Mother with the dishes, or complete their homework, or spend the money in their pockets for a new music book, but they find excuses for doing something else, and sometimes they are surprised to find that they have done exactly the opposite of what they intended. Not only the influence of their parents, but the strength of God is theirs for the asking, and they still do what no one wants them to do, not even themselves. This is a religious rather than an ethical problem. They know perfectly well what they ought to do, just as Paul did when he wrote that he wanted to do what he ought, but found himself doing the opposite. It is when the boys and girls come to this conclusion, that the Christian religion has an answer for them, "Thank God! it is done through Jesus Christ our Lord!" (Rom. 7:25,G).

It is not possible to give the boys and girls of this age a profound understanding of the meaning of the atonement, but they can see the connection in terms of forgiveness and grace. When a boy steals some ice cream and eats it, and then gets caught without the money with which to make restitution, he needs his father's help to get him out of this result of his sin. His father may forgive him when he confesses his misdeed, but the possibility of restitution is completely out of the boy's control unless the father provides the means and help necessary. When the consequences have been taken care of, it is then possible for the boy to be reinstated in terms of his relations with others, and his father can assist him in refraining from a similar situation. In one sense, but in terms of the whole of mankind, God paid in the death of Christ the price of men's sin, and thus set up the possibility of grace. So God works both through our own parents and through us directly to give us strength in the face of temptation. "Lead us not into temptation, but deliver us from evil," are phrases which will increase in meaning at this level of experience. This does not mean that God tempts us, but that we pray that by God's grace we may have power to resist temptation and the snares of evil found therein. In such a way as this, theology becomes relevant to the need for grace in the junior or intermediate boy or girl.

On the intermediate level, new means of grace are made available within the fellowship of the Church. In those denominations where confirmation is practiced, there is often a prayer for the gifts of the Holy Spirit. Confirmation not only involves the ratifying of baptismal vows, but "to confirm" means literally "to make firm" or to strengthen. The act of faith by the one being confirmed leads to the gifts of grace from God. The sustaining grace of God becomes available in a dependable way in so far as one fulfills or seeks to fulfill the vows of his baptism which have been reaffirmed at confirmation. In churches where confirmation is not a symbolic rite, the profession of faith prior to joining the church may have the same meaning and efficacy.

The problem is to make this experience real and vital to the adolescent age. They are not particularly in need of extra help, as they see it, because they are in the growing and expanding stage when no task seems too large for them to accomplish. Even at this stage, however, there are frustrations of which we take too little notice. Difficulties in adjusting to

school standards, inability to mix with their fellows, the beginning of dating, and growing independence of family ties are
serious problems. The Church offers to help them through its
worship, of which confirmation is the crucial experience, and
of which fellowship is a basic factor. This fellowship must
include not only companionship with other young people but
also a sense of being wanted in the adult congregation. Confirmation is a recognition of the beginning of Christian maturity, and too often the adults fail to realize this. From now
on, the boy or girl of twelve or more (and it is younger in some
churches) is received at the Lord's Table along with the older
members of his family, and assuredly Holy Communion is a
means of grace.

The strengthening and refreshing power of God's grace, as
received through continual practice of attending the Lord's
Supper, must be interpreted to the boy and girl in such a way
as to avoid disappointment. It is so easy to convince them to
expect a vivid experience of the presence of Christ at their
first communion (as at confirmation), and when there is no
great emotional upheaval, they will say that nothing happened. Perhaps those who are musically inclined may approach
the mystery of the sacrament in terms of learning to appreciate
a symphony. The first time a boy or girl hears a great symphony, there is likely to be little or no response in terms of
either emotion or appreciation. It takes time to come to an
understanding of what is being said through great music, but
there comes an experience when the whole person seems to be
attuned to the rhythms and melodies and variations of the
music and he desires to return to this experience over and over
again. While there is more of God's grace channeled through
the Holy Communion than through a symphony, involving
as it does the corporateness of a congregation, preparation for
reception, and an attitude of faith, one comes to appropriate
the values of the presence of Christ through constant exposure

to the Lord's Supper. There is a nurturing power about the atmosphere of worship and a contagion from the faith of other worshipers which build up channels of grace through the years. Christian experience testifies that the sacrament of the Lord's Supper is the surest means of grace given by God through his Church.

While intermediates will have some difficulties with appreciation of the Holy Communion, their eagerness to partake will give them spiritual values in spite of intellectual difficulties. They will be able to appreciate the need for self-examination as a prelude to receiving communion, they will understand why the Lord's Supper may not be celebrated by the officiant alone but only when at least two or three are gathered together in Christ's name, and they will begin to appreciate the power of God's grace and forgiveness which comes from regular reception.

The high school student will be more critical of some aspects of Holy Communion, especially as regards the "real presence" of Christ. Perhaps this illustration will help: "A dollar bill is not just an elaborately printed piece of paper, but has the value in currency of a silver dollar, which justifies us in speaking of it as 'a dollar.' In the same way, the bread and wine do not change substance, but they have the added value of Christ's spiritual presence." [9] Some of the communion hymns may be of assistance. The idea of Christ's sacrifice combined with the worshiper's gift of himself is admirably brought out in an old Greek hymn:

> "Thou didst die that I might live;
> Blessed Lord, thou cam'st to save me:
> All that love of God could give
> Jesus by his sorrows gave me.

[9] See my *Challenge of the Church*. New York: Morehouse-Gorham, student's book, p. 30; cf. William Temple, *Doctrine in the Church of England*. New York: Macmillan, p. 175.

Thou didst give thyself for me,
Now I give myself to thee." [10]

The meaning of joyful thanksgiving or Eucharist is illustrated in Horatio Bonar's hymn which begins,

"This is the hour of banquet and of song;
This is the heavenly table spread for me;
Here let me feast, and, feasting, still prolong
The brief, bright hour of fellowship with thee." [11]

Bonar's more familiar hymn shows the connection between communion with the Lord and eternal grace:

"Here, O my Lord, I see thee face to face;
Here would I touch and handle things unseen;
Here grasp with firmer hand th' eternal grace,
And all my weariness upon thee lean." [12]

The implications of the Holy Communion for Christian action must always be kept in mind. If we receive God's grace, it is for a purpose. We are strengthened and refreshed not only for our personal needs of body and soul, important as these may be, but also for the sake of society. High school and college students may discuss this with great value to their understanding of the significance and relevance of Christian worship. For example, the sharing of the bread and wine at the same altar rail or in the same pews stresses the equality of all who receive, and, because through the sacrament Christ is really present to everyone, all recipients are equally sons of God and joint-heirs with Christ. At the heart of the service, therefore, there is a reverence for personality regardless of race,

[10] *The Hymnal*, 1940, No. 190, 2nd stanza.
[11] *The Hymnal*, 1940, No. 206; *Christian Worship and Praise*, No. 600, stanza 3.
[12] *The Hymnal*, 1940, No. 208; *Christian Worship and Praise*, No. 600, stanza 1.

class, or sex based upon God's grace and not upon man's evaluation. "Christ died for you" refers to all who receive communion. The use of bread and wine, which are common necessities of life, imply that this common meal before God points to every man's right to the fundamental needs of food and lodging. The worshiping congregation is the family of Christ, and the fellowship before the Lord's Table must not stop at the Church door. The gifts of grace are for social reform as well as for reform of the individual. This can be understood by high school and college age worshipers, and it will enrich their worship and their Christian living.

The presupposition to all gifts of grace is faith. Faith may come by the preaching of the Word and the conviction of sin, with the resulting repentance and turning to God with trust; or faith may come through preparation for confirmation or joining the Church. In the sacrament of the Lord's Supper, "the mean whereby the body of Christ is received and eaten in the Supper is faith." [13] Thus, in any case, faith is the prelude to the receiving of God's grace, and to the problem of faith we shall turn in the next chapter.

[13] 18th Article of Religion, Methodist Church; 28th Article of Religion, Episcopal Church.

CHAPTER SEVEN
FAITH

I N one of his most delightful passages, William James
wrote, "What keeps religion going is something else
than abstract definitions and systems of logically concatenated
adjectives, and something different from faculties of theology
and their professors. All these things are after effects . . .
connecting themselves with feeling and conduct that renew
themselves *in saecula saeculorum* in the lives of humble private
men. If you ask what these experiences are, they are conversations with the unseen, voices and visions, responses to prayer,
changes of heart, deliverances from fear, inflowings of help,
assurances of support, whenever certain persons set their own
internal attitude in certain appropriate ways." [1]
The battleground of religious living is the area of faith
rather than belief, of experience rather than dogma, of grace
and forgiveness rather than creeds. But the theologizing which
James says is "after effects" is equally important, for we need
to know what faith is in order to guide our ways of living. We
have faith in a God we know, and this involves belief. Otherwise we are like the man whose passion for a certain lady was
perfectly charming except for the fact that the lady did not
exist. Faith involves relationship with a real person, and

[1] *Collected Essays and Reviews*, pp. 427-428, Copyright 1920 by Longmans, Green & Co. (New York) and used by their permission.

children can achieve this because of their trust in their parents.

Too often we mislead young Christians when they ask difficult questions by saying, "That is a matter of faith." If the reference is to a belief which seems absurd to them, they are going to be driven to the conclusion of the little boy who said, "Faith is believing what ain't true." There are times when faith is trusting far beyond the evidence, but then the evidence points in that direction. "Faith is the assurance of things hoped for, the conviction of things not seen" (Heb. 11:1,A). There are times when faith seems to contradict the evidence, but all the factors may not be in the equation.

I

Faith involves the whole man in his response to God. It is a total reaction, in which mind and will and emotions are integrated in devotion, trust and self-giving.

We begin with faith as an activity of the mind. Beliefs are essential guides to thinking and action, and no faith is worth holding if the beliefs are untrue. The great tragedies of modern times have been the almost noble faith that men have placed in objects and causes which do not deserve such unswerving loyalty. False messiahs, shallow political movements, and unjustified military causes may capture the imagination of men and stimulate their faith even unto death. The same kind of error has been made by Christians when they have refused to receive the truths established by modern science, Biblical scholarship, and philosophy. Wrong beliefs can lead to wrong action just as surely as right beliefs may direct right behavior. Beliefs become faith when they become guides to action, and "by their fruits shall ye know them."

Faith is never blind acceptance of authority, whether of Church or Bible. Faith is based on right beliefs. These beliefs arise from the evidence of what God has done for us and for all mankind. When we have faith in a friend or in a doctor, the basic element is trust, but it is trust to which all the evidence points; and when a doctor or a friend betrays that trust it also changes the evidence upon which our trust was based.

This does not mean that we establish our beliefs on reasonable grounds and then decide to have faith in the results. Faith in a real sense is prior to reason, and only as faith creates its own evidence can our beliefs be established. It is the act of faith which creates the data by which we may believe. Without faith, there is no grace in us, and without grace in us there is no evidence that our faith in grace for us is true. It is the analogy of friendship writ large, for only as we have faith in a friend may we discover his faithfulness; that faithfulness may be there, awaiting the opportunity to express itself, but the grace of friendship operates only when the faith is there to receive it. William James brings this out clearly in his classic statement on *The Will to Believe,* and he concludes, *"And where faith in a fact can help create the fact,* that would be an insane logic which should say that faith running ahead of scientific evidence is the 'lowest kind of immorality' into which a thinking being can fall. Yet such is the logic by which our scientific absolutists pretend to regulate our lives!" [2] Paul states the Christian answer to the rationalists when he writes, "Whatever does not proceed from faith is sin" (Rom. 14:23,A).

The emphasis on faith as involving the right use of the mind has led to the modern idea of *the* faith, as a body of truths or dogmas which must be accepted by the faithful. Both Roman Catholicism and Protestantism have established creeds, confessions, and formularies which summarize the doctrines of the faith. This obscures the personal relationship of Christian faith. It is perfectly proper to have a body of belief to which

[2] *Will to Believe.* New York: Longmans, Green, p. 25.

authority may be ascribed in various degrees, but this is not what faith means in the gracious personal acts of God in history and man's response to him. The traditional creeds use the phrase, "I believe *in*," rather than, "I believe *that*," and it is better to think of the creeds as professions of faith or symbols of loyalty rather than as outlines of dogma.

Faith involves right beliefs, but these beliefs, no matter how accurate, do not become faith unless they are guides to action. Faith is a response to God's grace *for* us, which is the prerequisite to God's grace *in* us.[3] Faith opens the doors to new evidence about God's nature which is simply not available to those who lack faith.

Faith is a matter of perspective. It is a way of looking at life with detachment and concern at the same time. Reinhold Niebuhr suggests a connection between faith and humor. When a man has the faith which triumphs over the incongruities and perplexities of life, his sense of humor will assist him in dealing with surface irritations and irrationalites, but unless it is grounded in faith humor will lead to despair in the face of ultimate issues. That is the pathos of "laugh, clown, laugh." "That is why there is laughter in the vestibule of the temple, the echo of laughter in the temple itself, but only faith and prayer, and no laughter, in the holy of holies." [4]

The object of faith is not a concept or a belief or a dogma. Faith for man is man's response to God's faithfulness. It is a personal relationship with man trusting himself to God. It is an answer to the good news revealed by Jesus Christ. The way into God's Kingdom is through faith.

To trust in a God of perfect goodness, who is the Father of Jesus Christ, involves a change in the one who trusts. He seeks to become like that Person. Repentance means a com-

[3] Cf. Harris Franklin Rall, *According to Paul*. New York: Scribners, pp. 58–65.

[4] Reinhold Niebuhr, *Discerning the Signs of the Times*. New York: Scribners, p. 131.

pletely changed outlook, a new perspective, a turning about. It is not moral change only, although it is primarily that; it is also a change in one's way of looking at his fellow creatures, at the society of which he is a part, at the Church, and at the whole creation. There is a new attitude, a new perspective, a new man.

This act of faith is completely free. Man is always free to reject the reconciliation which God offers him in Christ. Faith is a decision of the whole man to commit himself completely to God, to obey God's will, to see the world as God's world. To commit means to give one's self in trust, to place one's self in safe keeping, to pledge or bind one's self to a course of action.

Faith issues in a certain kind of action, which is dedicated to the holy will of Almighty God. There is no distinction between faith and works in the teachings of Jesus or Paul, except as Paul saw that the works of the ceremonial law were not due to faith. James's letter is a sound reaction against a misinterpretation of Paul's doctrine of "justification by faith," but when James wrote, "So faith by itself, if it has no good deeds to show, is dead" (James 2:17,G), Paul would have said, "but then it is not faith." Trust, repentance, and obedience are inseparable in faith. The Elder writes similarly: "And by this we may be sure that we know him, if we keep his commandments. He who says, 'I know him' but disobeys his commandments is a liar, and the truth is not in him; but whoever keeps his word, in him truly love for God is perfected" (I Jn. 2:3–5,A).

Faith centers in Jesus Christ. The profession of faith which the Church demands has always been, "Do you accept Jesus Christ as Lord and Savior?" In its various forms, this has always meant faith in what God has done through Christ for men. One form of this truth is expressed in the doctrine of justification by faith, which is the great emphasis of Pauline

Christianity. What Christ did and what man needs are here linked together. It is one thing to recognize that God was in Christ reconciling the world to himself, and it is another for men to have faith in God. What is important is that man trusts in God whose redemptive act was in Christ. The death of Christ does no man any good until it becomes part of man's approach to God.

Out of such faith comes "justification" or righteousness. Man, who cannot save himself, is enabled to become upright and is treated as upright by God. Therefore, man by faith becomes strengthened to do that which God makes possible.

Faith and grace are interacting in this experience. Man attains integrity or whole-ness by the grace of God when he has faith in the God who redeemed all mankind in Jesus Christ. It is an attitude of mind, an intention, which results in real ethical decisions which point in the direction of God's will. It does not lead to perfection (which is sanctification and not possible in this world), but to a personal relation to God and to men which is essentially right. This is more than goodness, more than repentance; it is a personality illuminated by the light of Christ, based on utter trust in him.[5]

As we shall show later, there are many things which men may do in the service of God, and thus there is no escape from moral and social responsibility. But what needs to be asserted time and time again is that any achievement of man in the service of God depends ultimately on man's faith in the redeeming grace of God in Christ.

Faith, then, involves right belief, commitment or trust, and action. No pious beliefs, no ceremonial, no moralism can take the place of an utter and complete trust in the Father of Jesus Christ, who by his grace gives us power to be repentant and obedient to him through the fellowship of his Church, and

[5] See Vincent Taylor, *Forgiveness and Reconciliation.* New York: Macmillan, pp. 56–82.

because we are creatures who are free, we will continue to be sinners and to need his continual grace.

II

The beginnings of faith in a small child are found in his relations to his parents. It is out of the security of the home and the confidence in his parents that the attitude of complete trust and devotion is developed. It is a long way from child-like trust in one's parents to mature faith in the God of Jesus Christ, for the object is entirely different, and yet Jesus likened the entrance to the kingdom of God to becoming as a little child. Whereas maturity is required as we put away childish things, we must not lose the transparency of childlike trust in what is trustworthy.

With this as a basic clue, we may assume that the child has a capacity for faith, although that faith may not be expressed in terms of the maturity of a poised and fearless Christian adult.

The security of the home is a primary consideration in building trust in God. The little child has some normal fears, especially of the dark, the bogey man, unusual noises, and strange people who force themselves upon them. He can be reassured by letting him know that God cares for him even when his parents are not watching him. This was the value of the first two lines of the old nursery prayer,

> "Now I lay me down to sleep.
> I pray thee, Lord, my soul to keep."

The new version continues:

> When in the morning light I wake,
> Help me the path of love to take,
> And keep the same, for thy dear sake. Amen."

Simple prayer habits at this time will begin the development of faith in a good God. The only danger is that even now the problems of unanswered prayer and of evil occurrences may upset the child's faith in God's goodness, unless some safeguards are set up to make it clear that everything is not too benevolent in nature and among men.

The kindergarten child needs the confidence of faith in God. He now has a dual center of loyalty, for although his mother is the center of his universe, he now has a teacher who supplies other emotional needs. The best safeguard against unreasonable fears is the happy home. He is afraid his mother will leave home, or not be home when he returns from school. He needs reassurance when his parents are out for the evening. He is not ready for the stimulation of fears in motion pictures, radio, and television, but he can learn to face up to fears when found in stories which are sound literature and which give additional meanings to his life. At Church school, he begins to learn about God at work in nature, and when he sees the growth of beautful flowers and healthy vegetables as God's work, with man's help always mentioned, he knows that God cares if he sees beauty and eats good food. He will ask many questions about God. He will share his parents' faith or lack of it, according to his limitations and his insights.

The primary child will need social assurance. He wants to be a member of the Church and know that he is recognized as such. At seven, he will like the Church's worship as an aid to his inner life. He will be sufficiently aware of death to ask questions about it. He will want to know where he stands in God's universe. Some believe that the primary child should be permitted to worship with the rest of the Church school in the Church, not because he can worship intelligently but because of the felt need of belonging to a body at corporate worship. By the third grade, he can read and sing well enough to be in the junior choir. The concept of God will have developed by this time so that he will have some idea of God's control of the universe. His questions will turn in the direction of almost impossible philosophical questions, such as "Where was God before he was born?" "Why did God let my puppy be run over?" "How did God get to heaven?"

Some of the better hymns will be helpful from kindergarten through the primary department, such as "All things bright and beautiful," which ends with that wonderful couplet:

> "How great is God Almighty,
> Who has made all things well." [6]

Third graders and juniors will like Jan Struther's hymn which describes God's place in nature, and ends with

> "For zeal and zest of living,
> For faith and understanding,
> For words to tell our loving,
> For hope of peace unending—
> We thank you, Lord, for these." [7]

Faith does things, and when the junior boy and girl begin their study of great Christian men and women, they begin to see the power of faith. The conclusion of a course on Old Testament heroes might involve a reading of the 11th chapter of the letter to the Hebrews, with the reminder that "God had foreseen something better for us. . . . Therefore, since we are surrounded by so great a cloud of witnesses, let us also lay aside every weight, and sin which clings so closely, and let us run with perseverance the race that is set before us, looking to Jesus the pioneer and perfecter of our faith, who for the joy that was set before him endured the cross, despising the shame, and is seated at the right hand of the throne of God" (Heb. 11:40; 12:1–2,A). This places the study of these

[6] *The Hymnal, 1940*, No. 311.
[7] *Ibid.*, No. 313.

great heroes and heroines on the proper level from the Christian perspective, and either the junior or intermediate boy or girl will get something of the meaning of faith from a creative use of this passage.

Another approach to faith at this period is through a study of friendship. Augustine long ago taught that Christian faith is not really other than the kind of faith we have in a friend or in a doctor. Our faith in the living Christ is like our faith in the friend whom we trust. God is the perfect Father, and if we can have faith in earthly fathers at their best, think how much more surely we can turn to God when we need him.

The emphasis on faith as trust can be illustrated with this bit of poetry, which would appeal to almost any age:

> " 'I have no faith in men,' you say:
> No faith in me, my eye!
> I saw you board a plane with ten
> And ride across the sky.
> 'I have no faith in God,' you wail:
> No faith in God indeed!
> Why did you dig into the sod
> And scatter flower seed?"

In this poem are the first glimmerings of the answer of God's grace. When a man by faith places seed in the ground, he must wait for the power of growth to bring that flower to bud. He can protect his plant from the cold, add fertilizer, and provide water, but the process of growing is not his. He may kill the plant, or he may stunt its growth, or he may prune it to change its direction and make it more bountiful, but each of these acts is a reflection of the amount of faith he has. Here certainly is a fundamental principle of the relation of faith and grace, of freedom and law, which boys and girls may apply to their own experiences.

At the high school level, a more challenging approach is

provided in a poem by Studdert-Kennedy. In strong language, written for soldiers, he says that he has to choose. Faith forces a choice upon him.

> ". . . I know not why the Evil,
> I know not why the Good, both mysteries
> Remain unsolved, and both insoluble.
> I know that both are there, the battle set,
> And I must fight on this side or on that.
> I can't stand shiv'ring on the bank, I plunge
> Head first. I bet my life on Beauty, Truth,
> And Love, not abstract but incarnate Truth,
> Not Beauty's passing shadow but its Self,
> Its very self made flesh, Love realised.
> I bet my life on Christ—Christ Crucified.
> Behold your God! My soul cries out. He hangs
> Serenely patient in His agony,
> And turns the soul of darkness into light." [8]

A discussion of this insight into the nature of faith could begin with Studdert-Kennedy's admission that he does not have all the answers, but that he sees the problems facing a valiant Christian faith. L. P. Jacks pointed this up when he wrote, "It is not the function of religion to answer all questions we raise in our perplexities. It is the function of religion to give a man courage to go in the face of life's perplexities." [9]

Faith involves the kind of decision we make when we stand beside a cold stream and then plunge into the waters. It takes courage, especially when it means betting one's life. And faith is just that, deciding to put one's self on the side of Christ and all that he stood for. And just as the cold waters startle

[8] *Rhymes*. London: Hodder and Stoughton, p. 13.
[9] L. P. Jacks, quoted in W. C. Barclay, *Challenge and Power*. New York: Abingdon, p. 111.

us into action, so God gives us power when we plunge in on his side.

A hymn like "My faith looks up to thee" tells of the forgiveness, grace, strength, zeal, and love which God makes possible in men. "A mighty fortress is our God" reminds us

> "Did we in our strength confide,
> Our striving would be losing;
> Were not the right man on our side,
> The man of God's own choosing."

Every college student should read William James' *The Will to Believe*, and especially the essay in that volume entitled "The Sentiment of Rationality," and within that essay is an illustration which may well be used on the high school level. James tells the story of being in the Alps, and, while he is climbing, he works himself into a position where the only escape involves a terrible leap. Having no evidence that he can make the jump, he has enough hope and confidence in himself to nerve his feet to do what would have been impossible without those subjective emotions. However, if we suppose that his emotions were those of fear and distrust (and that he felt it sinful to act upon an assumption without previous experience), he will hesitate so long and finally, in a thrust of despair, he will miss his foothold and fall into the abyss. In this case, his faith would create its own verification, while lack of it would prove the opposite.[10]

The learner at the age of confirmation can learn what faith in Jesus Christ as Lord and Savior is supposed to mean, but, as was pointed out in Chapter Two, it is difficult to establish the relevance of this faith and impossible for Christian nurture to bring it about. The experience of faith opens new vistas of Christian experience of the love of God, it gives serenity and security in the face of trial and tribulation, and it leads

[10] See *The Will to Believe*, pp. 96–97.

into the way of repentance and obedience constantly renewed by God's grace through worship and sacrament. It is relevant, because it is the sole means of a truly integrated personality in a world where devotion to ideals is not enough to construct a whole man.

A decision for Christ quite clearly means acceptance to full membership in the congregation, entrance to the sacrament of the Lord's Supper, and participation in the fellowship of the communion of faithful people. Only God knows when such an act of faith is genuine self-giving to him; the Church provides those channels of grace set up by God in the historical process by which men move toward salvation. Their faith is the precondition to any kind of grace, whether through Word or sacrament, and then God acts upon them in his own mysterious way. The twelve year old boy or girl does not know what is happening, but that does not preclude the occurrence. The channels of grace are open if God so wills.

Of one thing we may be sure. Unless the educational system of the Church brings boys and girls to the brink of the abyss, where they may make a decision for Christ and be saved or fall back and end up in the abyss, it is not a Christian system of education. Education at this focal point is evangelical or it is anti-Christ.

This has not been clearly seen by any of the educational philosophies of the past. There has been too much contentment with content, and too little progress with progressive methods to meet the real needs of the Church. The Church has a Gospel to proclaim which is the good news of Jesus Christ; its preaching is Christ and his relevance to every man; its theology is truth about God in relation to man, to boys and girls as well as to men and women; and its goal is to bring those under its care to the Christ; it is to expose them to the only true cure of souls which the world knows, and then, by the grace of God, in so far as the Church is the Church of

God, those who learn will make their decision to trust in God and commit themselves to him through Jesus Christ who died for them.

If the focal point of Christian education is Jesus Christ our Lord from the divine side, it is the response to him which is faith from the human side. "We live by faith," it has been said, and the nature of one's faith is determined by the object. There are competing faiths which seem almost to outrank Christianity in the world today, and there is a challenge in our culture which the Church has not yet faced. There is faith in science, which is a noble faith because it is given to the search for truth within experimental and rational limits. There is faith in man, which is noble when applied to man at his best, but the only example of man at his best is Jesus Christ and this points beyond to God. Otherwise, faith in man is a delusion and a snare, and this is the fundamental fallacy of all man-made ideals which capture the imagination and devotion of well-intentioned human beings. Faith in science and faith in man are the ruling philosophies in many of our schools, colleges, and universities. There is faith in many "isms" such as Communism, nationalism, capitalism, as well as the non-Christian religions. These ultimately fall short of the grace offered by faith in Christ, and our Christian education must make clear the options and the benefits of each. In many cases, it has been the failure of the Church which has enhanced the attractiveness of other objects of faith, especially Communism.

When Christianity is relevant and dynamic and truth-seeking, it has within it the best to be found in competing faiths, and it claims that it has *the way* of salvation. This claim can be defended and made attractive, and thus the power of Christ to redeem men will increase and more men by their faith will be justified by the grace of God.

There is no age when faith is irrelevant, but it is the faith of maturity toward which we strive, "reaching maturity, reaching the full measure of development which belongs to the fulness of Christ—instead of remaining immature, blown from our course and swayed by every passing wind of doctrine, by the adroitness of men who are dexterous in devising error; we are to hold by the truth, and by our love to grow up wholly unto Him" (Eph. 4:13–15,M). "For this reason, then," writes the author of the letter to the Ephesians, "I kneel before the Father from whom every family in heaven and on earth derives its name and nature, praying Him out of the wealth of his glory to grant you a mighty increase of strength by his Spirit in the inner man. May Christ dwell in your hearts as you have faith! May you be so fixed and founded in love that you can grasp with all the saints what is the meaning of 'the Breadth,' 'the Length,' 'the Depth,' and 'the Height,' by knowing the love of Christ which surpasses all knowledge! May you be filled with the entire fulness of God! Now to him who by the action of his power within us can do all things, aye far more than we ever ask or imagine, to him be glory in the church and in Christ Jesus throughout all generations for ever and ever: Amen" (Eph. 3:14–21,M).

CHAPTER EIGHT

PRAYER

PRAYER is not primarily a theological problem, but there is a theology of prayer, involving as it does the relations between God and man on a personal basis of communication.

Paul's admonition to the Thessalonians was "pray without ceasing" (KJ). Little children are more prone to accept this dictum than their parents, which is a sad commentary on our times. "Never give up praying" (G), "Pray perseveringly" (M), (I Thes. 5:16).

This is admittedly good advice and good theology, if we understand what it means. To some, perhaps, it means what it does to the Carmelite nuns who retire into a convent and never speak again to any man; they literally pray without ceasing. To others it may bring a reminder of the holy men of India, who develop techniques to keep them awake beyond the normal span in order to keep on praying. Most American Christians are very doubtful about the value or practicality of such prayer.

It is obvious that Paul did not have this extreme interpretation in mind. Paul did not waste his energy and was not over pious. He did not ask God to do for him what he ought to do for himself. Yet Paul was a man of prayer; he knew that he could do nothing without God's help; he constantly sought

God's guidance through the mind of Christ. So Paul could write, "Never cease praying. . . . Brothers, pray for us."

I

James Montgomery's great hymn tells us much about prayer, especially with the opening stanza:

> "Prayer is the soul's sincere desire,
> Unutter'd or expressed,
> The motion of a hidden fire
> That trembles in the breast." [1]

There is a negative side of prayer recognized in this stanza. There can be no prayer without desire, as is obvious in children's prayers. Unless a man really desires what he is praying for, it is not a true prayer. How often men's lips move to say "Amen" to some prayer in Church without realizing that this is an act of sincerity meaning "so be it." Is this what a man means when he hears the radical implications of the classic prayers: "fearlessly to contend against evil," "make no peace with oppression," "defend our liberties and fashion into one united people the multitudes brought hither out of many kindreds and tongues," "take away all hatred and prejudice and whatsoever else may hinder us from godly union and concord"? An old poem goes,

> "In prayer the lips ne'er act with winning part
> Without the sweet concurrence of the heart."

It is a question of complete integrity of purpose. "To pray," said the wise Archbishop Fenelon, "is to desire; but it is to desire what God would have us desire. He who desires not from the bottom of his heart, offers a deceitful prayer." [2]

[1] *The Hymnal*, 1940, No. 419.
[2] *Pious Thoughts: Advice Concerning Prayer*. Mrs. Mant's trans.

It is not possible to pray without desire, and those who profess to do so often end with the absurdity of the girl who prayed: "Dear Lord, I want nothing for myself; but please send my mother a son-in-law."

The desire behind prayer may be a great one or a small one. If it is sincere, that is enough. If it is true prayer, there will be an accompaniment to the melody of "Yearning," for the harmony will always repeat the basic rhythm of all prayer, "Thy will be done." If the desire is sincere, God will purify and correct it. "Anything large enough for a wish to light upon, is large enough to hang a prayer upon," said George Macdonald.[3]

Prayer arises in men's hearts because men need God. It arises as the response of men to the God in whom they live and move and have their being. Men pray because they cannot help it. They praise and adore him with their prayers, they grovel and writhe in the agony of their sins, they lift up their faces in repentance and confession, and their faces light up with the assurance of faith that absolution is theirs; they ask for what they truly desire for themselves and for others, and they receive the blessing of God's forgiving and power-giving grace.

Men pray because they cannot help it, but why? Here is God, who knows men's needs before they ask. Here is a loving Father, to whom men pray for the fulfillment of their own desires and yet in terms of God's will. Here is God who is perfect, and here are men who are imperfect, and yet men tell him what they think.

George Macdonald, who was one of the greatest inspirations for C. S. Lewis, poses the question and gives an unforgettable answer: " 'But if God is so good as you represent Him, and if He knows all that we need, and better far than we do

---

[3] *George Macdonald: An Anthology*, ed. by C. S. Lewis, p. 53 (No. 94). Copyright by The Macmillan Company and used with their permission.

ourselves, why should it be necessary to ask Him for anything?'
I answer, What if He knows prayer to be the thing we need
first and most? What if the main object in God's idea of
prayer be the supplying of our great, our endless need—the
need of Himself? . . . Hunger may drive the runaway child
home, and he may or may not be fed at once, but he needs his
mother more than his dinner. Communion with God is the
one need of the soul beyond all other need; prayer is the beginning of that communion, and some need is the motive of
that prayer. . . . So begins a communion, a talking with God,
a coming-to-one with Him, which is the sole end of prayer,
yea, of existence itself in its infinite phases. We must ask that
we may receive; but that we should receive what we ask in
respect of our lower needs, is not God's end in making us
pray, for He could give us everything without that: to bring
His child to His knee, God withholds that man may ask." [4]

When a child talks with his father, their relationship
deepens. The topic of conversation may be any subject from
philosophy to sport, but the important thing is that they are
in communication, and thus communion with each other. So
it is with prayer. We talk with God simply because he is our
Father. We need always to know that God is with us. John
Masefield put it beautifully when he wrote: "God warms his
hands at man's heart when he prays." [5]

Prayer is primarily an attitude which expresses itself primarily in a personal relationship between God and man. It is
an adjustment of man's personality to God's will. This interpretation of prayer needs to be carefully distinguished from
"having the right thoughts." We all know that men need
ideals for which to live. We build character around ideals,

[4] *Ibid.*, pp. 51–52 (No. 91).
[5] *Widow in the Bye Street*, from *Poems* by John Masefield, pt. vi. Copyright 1912, 1940 by The Macmillan Company (New York) and used with
their permission.

we devote ourselves to goodness, beauty, and truth. We integrate our personalities around the values of a culture. But this is not enough. A child can be trained in goodness, truth, manners, and poise. Teachers, tutors, and governesses may be hired to turn out well-behaved boys and girls. Yet there is something lacking in such a child; he does not have the spark which makes him truly a man; he does not show the fire which comes from love; he lacks the fundamental loyalty which comes from personal commitment. What he needs, and what every child needs, is the close relationship between himself and his parents, and in this atmosphere of loving care he will grow and mature.

> "And some I love have reached the end,
>   But some with me may stay,
>   Their faith and hope still guiding me:
>   I walk the King's highway." [6]

So it is with religion. We are reminded always that God is with us. Our ultimate security, our primary assurance, our basic faith are centered in the loving Father of us all, and not in creeds or cults or customs. The only way we can keep ourselves in that atmosphere is through prayer. The essence of prayer, then, is to know that we are in his presence. Then we will ask for nothing and in so doing ask for everything, for our desire will be to do God's will. The old Roman moralist, Seneca, born about the same year as Jesus Christ, put our petitions in the right order: "The first petition that we are to make to Almighty God is for a good *conscience*, the next for *health of mind*, and then of *body*."

So conceived prayer is not magic, not a "science of begging and getting from the gods," as Plato described it. It is not merely autosuggestion, although there may be something in this view of God at work through our minds. It is not a

[6] Evelyn Cummins, *The Hymnal*, 1940, No. 432.

substitute for works. It does not consist of certain words or postures or locations.

Prayer is primarily an adjustment, an attitude, an expression of desire, by which we come more fully into the presence of God, whom we cannot escape from even if we will do so. It is a "right religious adjustment," as Douglas Clyde Macintosh describes it. In this adjustment, there is power. God not only offers us knowledge of his will but also the power to do it. When we are in the right relationship with God, he gives us of his grace to know and to do his will.

This power of prayer is not only the power to do, but also it is the power to accept. Too often our prayers are statements of rebellion against what life has done to us. Yet there are many things in life which we cannot change. There are many hopes which are frustrated, many sincere desires which are never fulfilled, many dreams which are not realized. And when we face the inevitable and realize that there is nothing more that we can do to overcome obstacles, God gives us the help to see it through by accepting it.

When prayer gives us the power to accept what cannot be changed, that is not defeatism or pessimism. It is a form of realism which life demands of us. It makes what is necessary a burden which can be carried without bitterness.

The final gift of God's answer to prayer is not the power to overcome obstacles or the acceptance of the inevitable, but the wisdom to know which is which. In prayer, by the illumination of being in the presence of God, we can be saved from all false choices and preserved from faithless fears and worldly anxieties. Reinhold Niebuhr's prayer is a true summary of this view:

"O God, give us serenity to accept what cannot be changed; courage to change what can be changed; and the wisdom to know one from the other."

Paul was right when he wrote to the Thessalonians that they should "pray constantly." If prayer is our relationship with the Father of all mankind, if it is adjustment to the will of God, if it is an attitude by which we face all of life, there is no time when we are away from God. There is no time when he is inaccessible, no time when God is asleep, no time when we can afford to be without his power and strength and love. Prayer is not the words or the posture we use, and we cannot expect God to hear for our much speaking or our vain repetitions. Prayer is a conversation, but often a wordless one, in which both man and God have something to say. It is the awareness of God's presence which should never cease, and when our total beings reach out for God, he is there to help us in every situation.

When men have not developed the habit of praying without ceasing, they find themselves up against it when the time comes that prayer is necessary. There are many instances of men being in mortal danger, and then comes the gruesome question, "Can't anybody here pray?" Sometimes this works, but it is like asking a stranger for a favor. Not many people will ask an unknown person for the same help which their parents might readily give them. Children do not have the same faith in new acquaintances as in their parents. Yet there is a common procedure of calling on God at the last minute and asking him to pull a man's fat out of the fire. It is true that, because God loves men, it is never too late to turn to him, but God is man's Father and not a stranger, and therefore it is man's responsibility to keep in union with him even when life seems easy and without problems. Then, when life seems hard, it is natural to seek the power and help which God makes available in and through men.

The fundamental attitudes of prayer are expressed both in the experience of individuals and in the corporate worship of the Church. The basic elements are the same: adoration, praise, confession and repentance, listening, affirmation of faith, petition, intercession, and thanksgiving, with God's answer in terms of grace, which includes forgiveness, power, wisdom, and blessing.

The corporateness of public worship as compared with the privacy of the individual's prayer offers two aspects of the giving of ourselves to God. The corporateness of the Church is always a reminder that the people stand in a covenant relationship with God, and that through the Church God has provided special means of grace in its worship, preaching, and sacraments which are not available through any other means, although God is not limited by the institution which he has set up. Here is the group confessing that its primary concern is God rather than themselves. This congregational worship is the means to the power of the Church, for it is through worship that the Holy Spirit is truly given and received.

The prayer of the individual becomes the worship of the congregation, and this in turn becomes the prayers of the world-wide Church which is stronger than all the multitudes of groups at prayer. In so far as the Church becomes truly the Body of Christ, it has this power. But there can be no ecumenical worship, and no faithful congregation, unless the individuals in the communion of faithful people also know and speak with God in the privacy of their own souls.

The Church exists in the final analysis for only one thing: its great and unique contribution to man is its function as a congregation of faithful men, worshiping God in word and sacrament. All the faith of men's response to God, and all of God's free grace for men, are centered in the great acts of worship in the Church. The Church always points beyond itself to God who willed it, just as the creatures who constitute the congregation of Christ's Church point beyond themselves to the Creator.

Christian education, in bringing its learners to accept Christ as Lord and Master, seeks also to make them members of the Body of Christ which is his Church. Thus the theology of worship becomes relevant to the life experience of everyone who would be saved, and truth-about-God underlies the Christian educational process at this crucial point as at all others.

II

Children can pray, because prayer is an attitude toward God, and since prayer is man's response to the vision of God much of the meaning of prayer depends on one's concept of God. The child's introduction to the word and concept of God usually begins with his earliest prayer habits. If his idea is of God as "a friend for little children above the bright blue sky," his attitude of prayer will reflect this concept. The small child will not comprehend many of the mysteries of God, but he will accept many ideas which seem baffling to his parents.

It is not hard for a small child to think of an invisible God, for he already has his unseen playmates and perhaps one of them will be named "Jesus." He is able to imitate his parents' attitudes of reverence (or lack of it) when grace is said at mealtime. When he goes to nursery class at Church school, he and his friends will have times when prayer will be offered.

Many books of prayers for small children have been written in recent years. These prayers often reflect the experiences of real children, and others illustrate how children might like to pray. The earliest prayers will sometimes be simple expressions of gratitude, such as "thank you, God, for today's picnic and the games and little sister. Make me a good boy. Amen," with the latter phrase being Mother's attempt at autosuggestion in prayer. At meals, the children will join in the grace, take turns leading it, or make up their own.[7]

[7] See Dora Chaplin, *Children and Religion*, pp. 57–61, for examples; also Harold Burdekin, *A Child's Grace*, for the very young.

Great care must be taken in interpreting the meaning of prayer to all children, for it is easy for them to get mistaken ideas and lose all faith in prayer. Unsubstantiated claims of the power of prayer often lead to asking prayers, for dolls to be fixed, bicycles to be given, grandmothers to get well, and when the prayer is "not answered" faith is lost. There is no way of stage-managing this, for a child will often pray in secret and thus cannot have his prayer intercepted in the way his parents obtain his letters to Santa Claus. Even a simple prayer, "Make me a good boy," may lead to frustration when it is followed by a worse case of disobedience than usual.

A more objective type of asking prayer is when it is for others. Even here there may be disillusionment, for puppies and friends do not always get well; and the Chinese do not often get enough food; and even when they do the prayer may be a substitute for works.

In all attitudes of prayer, it is sincerity which counts much, and verbalization may not always be sincere. The frustrations of unfulfilled petitions may be sincere, but some children say their prayers to watch the effect on their parents, for it may prove a way out of a difficult situation. The "I'm sorry, God" type of prayer is sometimes of this sort.

Children are also smart enough to use "guidance" for their own benefits if their teaching is poor. "I prayed, and God told me I could," is usually too sophisticated a trick for a small child, but in homes where "guidance" is uncritically accepted it makes a valuable weapon for a foxy youngster.

Many times wise parents can guide a child's thoughts by conversation. It may not seem like prayer to those who insist on a formal address to God, but often a talking through of a problem may conclude with an agreement to do better next time, or change one's whole mode of behavior. A poem or reading from certain stories may inculcate a prayerful attitude.

The formal prayers said at bedtime may easily be pure repetition, and it is the experience of most of us that there comes a time in every child's life when he wants to say his prayers privately or to himself, and it is not long before prayer ceases to be a habit. How to maintain a prayer habit after parental supervision ceases is not easily answered, but it helps if there is grace at meals and if prayer is also a habit with the parents.

What needs to be understood is that the attitude of prayer may not be expressed in words. Often the most effective prayers are in terms of thoughts and desires which are not expressed. A sense of communion with God is sometimes the result of a momentary silence, when the child sees the meaning of "Be still; and know that I am God." There is an undercurrent of faith which runs through his daily life, and he is dimly aware of the grace of God as he goes about his tasks. Such a child is not at a loss for words when he needs them, words which may come spontaneously from his heart or words which are part of his subconscious and have been assimilated by his memorizing of great devotional passages.

The Lord's Prayer serves a dual purpose. It provides the classic example of every attitude of prayer without much speaking. It is, when properly taught, too incisive to be parroted. It serves as a basis for discussion of what prayer may mean at any age level, even when the four year old asks, "Mommy, what's *dailybread*?" But it is a prayer of fellowship, and by knowing the words the child is included in the body of worshipers. The smaller children in the home join with the older children and parents, and know that they belong religiously to the company of believers. The Lord's Prayer serves this same function liturgically, for in Church school the one prayer every child should know is this great one. Thus, even when the words are almost meaningless, he knows that he is a member of Christ's Church and can say Jesus' prayer with all the other children and adults. This sense of corporateness is often the child's introduction to the Church's worship.

The worship of the Church school should take its clue from this use of the Lord's Prayer. One of the important aspects of Church school worship is the sense of fellowship at worship. Attitudes are more important than meanings, at first, although both meaning and attitudes will be goals of corporate worship.

There is division of opinion about closely graded worship. There are some who favor departmental worship, with the emphasis on meaning. There are others who prefer worship in the Church, with the emphasis on attitude and with meaning of significance but not of primary importance. If this second view is accepted, it follows that except for the smallest children, there will be a "junior church" worship modelled after "senior church." Its psychological and liturgical order will be the same as adult worship, but it will be graded for both meaning and atmosphere to reach the "growing edge" of the learners.

The selection of prayers, Bible lessons, and hymns will be in terms of both meaning for the children and growth in appreciation of the classical forms of worship. Thus the Lord's Prayer will be used, and the 23rd Psalm, along with simpler writings of as great beauty as possible. "Jesus, tender shepherd, hear me," will be used, and so will "Holy, holy, holy." Thus we do not get lost in the limitations of childhood and do not sell out to maturity. This is not a compromise, but a recognition of the need for both atmosphere and meaning in worship. When the child is through with "junior Church" he should feel at home already in "senior Church." Thus worship will include all the psychological attitudes at every level.[8]

There will also be the study of the meaning of prayer and worship. This must be theologically based, for we must know

[8] See my *Guide for Church School Teachers*. Chicago: Wilcox & Follett, (Cloister Press), pp. 59-70.

who is this God whom we seek in our sincerest desires. The nursery children will have questions, and the answer must be in terms of their concepts of God. "How loud do I have to shout for God to hear me?" "How can he hear me if I don't say it out loud?" "What's the good of yapping the same thing at God every night?"

An elementary study of the Lord's Prayer is possible at the third grade level, along with an introduction to the worship of the Church. In both cases, the units would be brief and part of a general study of the Church or of the way Christians act.

Before confirmation, there needs to be careful study of these subjects on the sixth grade level, looking forward to the boy's or girl's reception of the Lord's Supper. Here there will be difficulties of language, for all Communion services are in terms of Biblical theology. We have discussed this more fully in the chapter on Grace.

The high school and college age will be skeptical, and will ask, "Does prayer work?" The approach through prayer as an attitude will overcome most of their objections, for usually the skepticism is based on unanswered petitions. Let us admit that *magic* is "the science of begging and getting from the Gods," and recall Plato's other statement that worse than atheism is the belief that the Gods can be bribed. Then prayer may be seen as the "soul's sincere desire" as "not my will but thine be done." Prayer is primarily being in the presence of God, and by the faith expressed in prayer we receive grace to face and overcome some obstacles, to be comforted in the face of the inevitable, and to attain insight into God's truth. This places prayer on an adult basis, and a study of the Lord's Prayer will reveal the basic attitudes which should be expressed. Certain hymns dealing with prayer or expressing prayerful attitudes might be examined, especially "Prayer is the soul's sincere desire," "Dear Lord and Father of mankind,"

"The king of love my shepherd is," and "O God of earth and altar, bow down and hear our cry."

Prayer is never a substitute for works, but it may provide the motivating spirit for our deeds. Prayer is a means whereby God works through us, and it opens doors of God's power which otherwise would be closed to him and to us.

Olive Wyon tells a beautiful story which has been extremely effective with high school students. She tells of a man who dreamed he was in a Church. After he had finished his prayers, he remained kneeling and admired the beauty of the ancient building. He watched a little white bird flying uncertainly, almost falling once or twice to the ground. Finally, it seemed to gain a sense of direction and sufficient strength, and it swept upward and out one of the windows into the sunshine.

As he looked around, he saw a number of worshipers, each with a little white bird beside each of them. Another rose from the floor, flew around in circles, and tried to go through the lower windows which were sealed; it finally became exhausted and lay still.

After a while, another bird swiftly and easily went toward the sunlight, and it seemed as if he would make it, when it suddenly whirled and dropped to the ground as if it were shot. The man curiously walked over and saw that the bird was dead.

An ugly little bird, dirty and bedraggled, was next. He labored heavily at first and his take-off was not graceful, but he was strong and he gathered speed and soared straight into the sunlight.

The dreamer saw a very beautiful bird lying beside a man who knelt reverently. He wondered at the stillness of the bird, and as he looked more closely he saw that its eyes were glazed and its wings stiff. It had no life at all.

Then a bird's gentle whirring caused him to watch as it rose with some effort and then move lightly as it gathered speed. "This bird flew straight up, past the carved angels that seemed to be crying 'Hallelujah!' to one another across the dim spaces of the Church, and out through the open window into the blue sky, where it was soon lost to sight."

The man was perplexed, and as he wondered he saw an Angel, of whom he asked, " 'Can you explain to me about these white birds?'

" 'Yes,' said the Angel, 'for I am the guardian of this place of prayer. These white birds are the outward sign of the prayers of the people who come here to pray. The first bird, which found it difficult to rise, is the prayer of a woman who has come here, straight from her busy life; she has very little time to herself; in fact, she usually comes here in the midst of her shopping. She has a great many duties and claims, and her mind was full of distractions when she first knelt down and tried to pray. But she persevered, for her heart is right with God, and he helped her. Her prayer was real and her will was good, and so her prayer reached God.'

" 'And what about the bird that flew around in circles?' asked the man.

"The Angel smiled slightly, with a tinge of faint amusement. 'That is the prayer of a man who thinks of no one but himself; even in his prayer he asks only for "things"—success in his business and things like that; he tries to use God for his own ends. People think he is a very religious man, but his prayer does not reach God at all.'

" 'But why did that other bird fall to the ground as if he had been shot?'

"The Angel looked sad as he replied, 'That man began his prayer well enough; but suddenly he remembered a grudge against someone he knew; he forgot his prayer and brooded in bitter resentment, and his bitterness killed his prayer.

" 'And the ugly little bird,' he went on, 'is the prayer of a man who hasn't much idea of reverence; his prayer is bold,

almost presumptuous some people might call it. But God
knows his heart, and he sees that his faith is real; he really
does believe in God, and so his prayer reaches him.'

" 'And the beautiful lifeless bird that never stirred from the
ground at all?' asked the man.

" 'That,' said the Angel, 'is a beautifully composed prayer.
The language is perfect, the thought doctrinally correct. The
man offered it with the greatest solemnity and outward reverence. But he never meant a word of it. Even as he said the
words, his thoughts were on his own affairs. So his prayer
could not reach God.'

" 'And what about the last bird that flew upwards so easily?'

"The Angel smiled. 'I think you know,' he said gently. 'That
is the prayer of a woman whose whole heart and will is set
upon God. Her prayer went straight to God.' " [9]

A final question asked by many young people is, "Why do
we have ceremony and ritual in worship?" The ceremonials
are the outward forms of worship and exist to provide the
actions which make it possible for a congregation to worship
decently and in order. We sit and stand and kneel as a group
to express fundamental religious attitudes. Visual aids are provided in the Church's architecture, the altar, the use of sacraments, and vestments. These ceremonials may be changed at
any time, and different ceremonials are popular in various
denominations and among the congregations of the same
denomination. They have grown up in the experience of various groups and exist to make worship more corporate in
nature. Unfamiliar ceremonial seems artificial, and almost
always questions of young people are based upon lack of
acquaintance and experience with a particular form of worship.
However, these ceremonial practices come to have meanings

[9] Olive Wyon, *The School of Prayer*. Philadelphia: Westminster Press,
pp. 15-18.

and associations. When a Roman Catholic makes the sign of the cross, it is a manual act of deep devotion, while for the non-conformist who observes him it is sheer superstition or popery. When a choir vests, it is for the purpose of preserving anonymity, but for the non-vesting groups it seems like showing off. The same difference of opinion surrounds placing a cross on the Lord's Table, using candles on the altar, kneeling, and bowing at the name of Jesus.

Ritual, as distinguished from ceremonial, concerns the words used. The purpose is the same in each case: to provide for congregational worship. There is as much ritual in a free service following a service sheet as in a service drawn from sources in a book. The use of written prayers is no more ritualistic in this sense than use of extempore prayers; it is only "more liturgical" in that different means are used for providing the corporateness of worship. The churches which use "collects," for example, are using prayers written for the specific purpose of being read aloud in a service of worship. They are a form of rhythmic prose, containing a single thought, and usually are extremely brief. An almost perfect example of a collect is the following from the Gregorian Sacramentary of the seventh century:

> "Almighty God, unto whom all hearts are open, all desires known, and from whom no secrets are hid; cleanse the thoughts of our hearts by the inspiration of thy Holy Spirit, that we may perfectly love thee, and worthily magnify thy holy Name; through Jesus Christ our Lord."

The purpose of ritual, like that of ceremonial, is to provide a familiar atmosphere in which the worshiping congregation may attain the fundamental attitudes of worship. They are aids to worship and have no value in themselves, but they have been set up by the Church out of its experience as the best means available. The goal is always the worship of Almighty God.

Worship is life-centered education at its best, for in the worship of the Church the learner is in the presence of God, and thus there is the opportunity for the development of faith and the receiving of grace.

CHAPTER NINE

BEHAVIOR

THE grace we receive in the congregation of the faithful is for a purpose. Jesus said that men would be known by their fruits. Paul never conceived of faith without works, and if anyone should misunderstand him at that point, the letter of James serves as a reminder that "faith without works is dead." The opposite danger is to attempt works without faith, and it is the emphasis on ethics without theology which has led such continental theologians as Karl Barth to suggest that American Christianity is "boring," because it is so interested in "activism" that it fails to be grounded in God.

What has happened in theology and Christian ethics is a realization that all Christian behavior must be placed in the religious dimension. Thus moralism and the subsequent talk of "building" the kingdom of God have dropped from the vocabularies of theologians and educators alike. The Christian ethic is a religious ethic, and all activity is centered in faith in God. Faith is the basis of justification; and without grace we can do nothing. The relevance of theology for behavior is made abundantly clear, for the only behavior which is Christian is that which comes from the will of God as he works out his purpose in and through men. The implications of this view for the character education of children, both in the home and in the Church are enormous.

I

We need to think of Christian behavior first of all in terms of discovering and doing the will of God. The Christian is a baptized member of the Body of Christ, and thus the framework of all his ethical decisions is provided by the Church, with its sources of authority. The specific problem of authority will be faced in a later chapter, and here it is only necessary to say that all Christians recognize the primary place of the Bible and especially the New Testament as interpreted in terms of "the mind of Christ."

When it comes to specific ethical decisions, however, the appeal to the Bible offers difficulties. The authority of the Bible is always in terms of the Bible-as-interpreted-by-groups-of-individuals. There needs to be a point of reference by which the ethical principles of the Bible may be evaluated, and the focal point of Jesus Christ as seen in "the mind of Christ" offers the best available information, for it at least has the objective validity of the teachings of Jesus as found in the Synoptic Gospels.

Appeal to the authority of the Church offers equal difficulty. There are even more points of view in the Church than in the Bible. Many of the official teachings on various questions are different for every denomination and often for congregations within the denomination, where some rulings may be found in minor matters which seem to be of practically no ethical importance. Furthermore, many "official" statements by intelligent leaders are not acceptable to the secularized ethical minds of lay people.

The individual, with his own faith, makes his own choices between the possibilities opened to him by the Bible, the Church, and his own experience. In the last analysis, the individual must make the decision and live with his own con-

science, but his conscience is even less likely to be reliable than
the Bible or Church. Conscience, which is far from infallible,
must rely on the insights of others, especially in the Church
and Bible, which are not infallible either, and thus the de-
voted, sincere and seeking Christian is caught in a vicious circle
of relativity. If he lacks the courage to stand on his own feet
before God, he falls back on Church and Bible, and thus is
guilty of absolutizing views which can be shown to be relative.
This is simple idolatry, however noble it may be, for it substi-
tutes something less than deity for God himself. But if he
insists on remaining an individualist, he loses the resources of
the group and tradition, and is in danger of absolutizing his
own ideas, which are even more relative than those of the
groups he has rejected.

If the ethical question is answered on purely ethical grounds,
there will be no satisfactory answer, for the basis of ethics is
the will of the living God and not a set of ideals. The chief
power of the Church, as we have tried to show, is that it has a
Gospel. The good news of Jesus Christ, who came from God
to save, redeem and reconcile men, puts salvation on a plane
higher than ethics. Just because there was an incarnation, we
know that God is at work in the world, and whenever God's
will is translated into human terms, it ceases to be absolute and
becomes permeated with the relativities of human experience.
The worshiping community of the Church universal places the
relationship to God in terms of faith, which is personal and
not legal, and God's grace gives men power to do his will for
them in a specific situation. The absolute will of God, which
transcends men in their historic situation, stands in judgment
while men respond to God in faith. This provides a tension for
ethical living which is illustrated in two quotations. The first
is a great commandment of Jesus which is also the height of
religious irony: "You, therefore, must be perfect, as your
heavenly Father is perfect" (Mt. 5:48, A). This is true, but it

must be kept at the proper state of tension with the other admission: "Why do you call me good? No one is good but God himself" (Mk. 10:18, G).

Various attempts are made to equate levels of goodness with the will of God. The solution found in most Church school lesson materials is that the will of God is simply the best one can do in any particular situation. This means building up a system of ideals, or dreaming of a Utopian society. It is the error of the Roman Church in equating itself with the kingdom of God on earth. It is the error of Protestants who identify the kingdom with some ethical, social, or political system. What happens is that the basic tension between God and his creatures is lost.

Another interpretation is to make the ethics of the New Testament irrelevant. This happens when it is called an "interim" ethic, or an ethic for the future kingdom, or when it is applied to individuals and not to the State. It becomes dangerously close to irrelevance when its impossibility is so emphasized that there is complete discontinuity between what God requires and what man does.

Theology provides an answer to man's ethical dilemma. It is true that God is absolute, and his will is perfect. But God also expresses his will in history, and the Holy Spirit, whatever else he may be, is God immanent, at work in the world and in us. Thus God's will becomes relevant to the human situation. Man does not achieve God's absolute will, but there is continuity between what man can do and what God requires, and thus man may *approximate* God's will for him.

The man who is committed absolutely to God's will seeks to discover through every tool at his command the potentialities of value which are really in his power, and to decide how he best can open himself in faith to God's working and God's power through him. These decisions are of many kinds. Some are simple choices between two or more good acts. Some are even simpler choices between good and bad acts, although his tendencies to follow his own pleasures may corrupt his commitment; and even if he is successful in keeping his motives pure and his actions good, the tension is not lost because he sees how far short he falls of being what God wants him to be. Then there are those tragic situations where he can only choose the lesser of two evils, because no other alternative is open to him. Simply by being in society, he faces possibilities which are relatively evil. Furthermore, when he chooses good and knows it, he may have his decision corroded by pride in his achievement and may forget that God's grace made it possible. It is no accident that the "saints" were always aware of their sins.

The Christian ethic is always directed to the will of God, rather than to any ideal, even the ideal of love, for it is a religious ethic. Christian behavior is achieved among men by God's grace. Man's own seeking after his own highest ideals leads to moralism and not to a religious ethic. The Christian ethic finds its dynamic power through the absolute commitment of the self to the will of God. It is a religious relationship which results inevitably in ethical action. The coming of the kingdom is God's act and not man's; man fulfills the conditions, but it is the religious dimension which is prior to the ethical.

Certain limited standards are drawn from the Biblical revelation of God in Jesus Christ which help men of faith to direct their actions along the lines of God's will. The first of these, a command "equal" to the prior command to love God, is to "love his neighbor as himself." This implies that he should treat every person as an end and never as a means, although the Christian may use himself as a means. There is no "greatest good of the greatest number," for the minority left out of such a calculating equation is equally valuable in God's sight. There can be no classless society by eliminating certain classes but only by transcending them. There can be no freedom for "believers" only, but for all the children of God. No congregation should mark itself off as "interracial," for no Christian Church can be otherwise where there is "neither Jew nor Greek." The Christian Church seeks to deal with the whole man in his total environment, and when the Churches fail to reach this goal they are equally under the judgment of God.

While the Golden Rule is too subjective to be a dependable guide to action, the admonition, "As ye would that men should do to you, do ye also to them likewise" (Lk. 6:31, KJ), adds guidance to the command to love one's neighbor. There is a demand here for empathy, for seeing the world through the eyes of the other, before the Golden Rule is relevant.

Further interpretation of Jesus' commandment is found in the kind of society Christians demand. It is to be a society in which every *child* will receive his due, where justice is interpreted in terms of need and opportunity, where there will be sufficient freedom and fellowship for the maturing of every person. It means that the earth's resources are to be used as gifts of God rather than as property of vested interests. The Christian, therefore, is not bound by the restrictions and interests of secular, economic, industrial, or political standards, and although he will be loyal to his nation, he may represent a loyal opposition.

Properly to provide conditions under which the Christian ethic may be practiced, the Christian requires a certain amount of political and social liberty for the Church, so that the Church may seek its own announced goals. The Church has been forced under ground in some countries, has been banned in others, and is not free to be Protestant in countries where the Roman Church controls the policies of religious freedom.

All of these Christian standards of judgment are general, but they point in the direction of God's will for men and nations. The expediting of them in particular situations involves the powers of critical judgment and the courage of positive action, and this in the last analysis comes down to the motives of individual men. The Christian's behavior is not based primarily on standards, but on an inner attitude of faith. His intentions, loyalty, and devotion are more significant that his proclamations of ideals. "Is thine heart right?" asked John Wesley, and only by such a question does a man escape the danger of hypocrisy. "Here I stand. I can no other. God help me. Amen," said Martin Luther, and only by such steadfastness in the face of political and ecclesiastical opposition will men move forward toward God's will for them. "Be of good comfort, Master Ridley, we shall this day light such a candle, by God's grace, in England, as I trust shall never be put out," said Bishop Hugh Latimer, and only by such sacrifice will the light of the glory of God be continued in this world.

The calm understatement of the *Book of Common Prayer* takes on fuller meaning against this background: "My bounden duty is to follow Christ, to worship God every Sunday in his Church; and to work and pray and give for the spread of his kingdom." The beginning of Christian behavior is as a member of Christ's Church, where man accepts Jesus Christ as his Lord and Savior, and then follows him with whatever light the grace of God may grant him. It is in the crucible of the worship and fellowship of the congregation that faith is nurtured and grace is given, so that men may become "climbers of the steep ascent." "To work and pray and give for the spread of his kingdom" is not limited to life with the worshiping fellowship, for the Church is not only fellowship but also those who are "called out" to do God's will in his world, and the Kingship of God means that he reigns over all that he has made. There are no limits to Christian ethics when we pray, "Thy kingdom come, thy will be done on earth as it is in heaven." There is no faith without works, no worship without action, no Christianity without ethics, no indi-

vidual duties without social responsibilities, no reborn creatures without a reborn creation, no Gospel without a social
Gospel.[1]

II

The problems of Christian ethical decisions face the little
child at an early age. The responses to situations built into his
habits by his parents at the earliest age determine much that he
does by choice as he grows older. The earliest experiences
within the unit of the family on a day by day basis provide
personality traits and behavior patterns before the child can
articulate them. The fundamental needs of a child's emotional and spiritual life must be met as dependably as his
physical needs. Parents often do not realize this, and in their
own instability provide an environment which the child finds
not only confusing but utterly unpredictable. Other parents,
knowing the need for discipline, dependability, affection, and
confidence, are able to create an atmosphere in which the
child may grow naturally and with greater ease toward a fuller
and richer personality.

It is not long before a child from even a smooth running
family will experience confusion of standards. The playground
or the nursery school puts up a challenge immediately when
he comes in contact with children who have been taught to
react differently to situations. The child who does not have to
fight for his rights at home faces a major catastrophe when
another child takes away his rights and defends them with
force if necessary. The timid child is often ashamed when he
meets competition on the slide or with blocks. If his security
in the home has been a cushioned security, he is going to have

[1] Some material in this section is based on my article, "The Relevance of
Christian Ethics," *Religion in Life*, XIV, pp. 205-215; and *The Church
and Organized Movements*. New York: Harpers, pp. 3-25.

a rough time establishing a new kind of security outside the home; but if he has security based upon interaction with persons and in terms of developing resources for meeting problems, a new problem will enrich rather than destroy his sense of security.

The first time a child is faced with the temptation of not telling his parents what happened is typical of this kind of experience. Two children are wondering whether to report what happened at nursery school, where there was a fight. One says: "I'll tell Mommy." The other says, "Why don't you say you fell down?" The difference in family background is immediately apparent.

The first time a child comes up against an unpleasant school situation and reports it to his parents, may also be crucial. It may seem obvious to the parents that a teacher has been unfair, but the answer is not to sympathize with the child and build a spirit of antagonism; the answer is to lead the child to solve the problem of getting along with his teacher. A negative reaction to Church school should be handled in the same fashion. The task is to give children the kind of personality which is able to adjust to the personalities of others, however clashing the relationship may at first seem. To adjust is not to submit, but to seek a creative relationship.

Temperamental music teachers may serve as an example. Two boys were disciplined for their behavior at choral rehearsal. Both came home indignant at the high-handed behavior of the teacher. One boy's parents suggested that he should decide which course of action was better: to stay angry and not learn to sing, or to return and try to obey the conductor. He made his choice and learned not only to sing but a lesson in personality adaptation. The other boy's parents were indignant, made scathing remarks about the teacher, encouraged the boy's animosity, and protected him from further experiences of the kind.

Training in Christian character involves the home at every stage of growth. The Church cannot accomplish very much by itself, for the behavior pattern of one hour a week cannot determine the other hours. With the cooperation of parents who seek to inspire the same kind of behavior the Church calls for, much growth in character may be observed. The most thorough-going experiment of this sort is the Character Education Project of Dr. Ernest Ligon,[2] where parents work with the Church on Sundays and during the week.

The relevance of the Christian religion to every aspect of life is illustrated at every age-level as far as Christian behavior is concerned. The child is unable to think in terms of "the good," and if an adult thinks this abstract term is easy to define let him try to write a definition of "goodness." The good must always be "good for something" and the purpose of the Christian religion is to know and do what God wants.

Just as in the history of the race, the child learns at first through laws. There are the commands of his parents, the discipline of school precedures, the laws of society. He early knows what is forbidden, even though he may deliberately go against it. The Ten Commandments are too vague for a small child, but by the time he is in the junior department he knows what all of them mean, except the one about adultery. It is through the discipline of law that one comes to the freedom of faith, and this is as true for children as for the tribes of Israel.

Dean de Ovies, in *The Church and the Children*, presents in a brilliant way the problem of developing ethical discrimination in juniors. He takes a problem and presents it as a story which in no way involves the children who are listening but which is so likely an experience they could have that they throw themselves wholeheartedly into the problem. An ethical problem comes before the boy or girl in the story, and then

[2] See Ernest Ligon, *A Greater Generation*. New York: Macmillan.

temptation is dealt with in some detail as the suspense mounts. Possible alternatives to the right answer are considered by the central character in the story, and the listeners are able to make an objective evaluation because they are not personally involved. This approach avoids scolding or nagging or putting the listener on the defensive. A variation used by the Dean is to divide the class into boys and girls, present a boy's problem for the girls to solve and then immediately a girl's problem for the boys to solve. By the appeal to imagination, the answers are made vivid enough to be transferred to actual experiences in the present and the future. Frequently, the story is related to an experience in the Bible, and a successful temptation story could be related to Jesus' temptations while unsuccessful facing of temptation, followed by repentance, could be related to the Prodigal Son, and the pride of not yielding to temptation and being a hypocrite could be related to the Elder Son.[3]

A series of "Right or Wrong" problems as a basis for discussion can be handled by a creative teacher, with the boys and girls of about intermediate age presenting the problems to be solved and then discussing the possible answers. There are many problems, and the discussion of them will be illuminating. The use of the Ten Commandments for evaluating conduct at any junior high school will show that while the commandments are accepted as a basis for behavior, every one of them will be broken in the course of a school year, although murder is rare but not unheard of. Cheating is a common practice, "because it is the only way to pass in a class graded on the curve where eighty per cent of the class cheat." (This reasoning is used by all ages from junior high school through graduate school.) Lying to a teacher or parent is often justified on the basis that to tell the truth means undeserved punishment and adults are too dumb to find out the truth otherwise.

Problems are everywhere for the high school age. They have

[3] See *ibid.*, pp. 120–126.

difficulties with their parents. Some homes are divided, others are indifferent, and the rest do not understand adolescent problems. Young people from homes where dancing, smoking, motion pictures, and card playing are frowned upon feel a great tension when they must adjust to a society which approves these things. Repressive religion breaks out in all kinds of less healthful recreation. Too little supervision from parents leads to another set of dangers, and the interests and standards of "the crowd" are easily accepted. Social pressures convince the young girl that she must "neck" to be popular, and smoking and liquor are introduced at teen-age parties.

Where the religious background provided by home and Church is "healthy-minded," to use William James' phrase, the tension is between what a young person is and what he ought to be. This is a natural strain on the conscience, for it puts the emphasis on achieving higher values. This approach to religion appeals to the high school youngster in his ethical dilemmas, for he is more interested in achieving good than in escaping evil.[4]

The major emphasis in determining Christian behavior is to increase the ethical discrimination of the learner at every age level. Ethical judgments are grounded in theology, for "the good" is meaningless without reference to God. Sheer ignorance of what is good or bad is one of the great weaknesses of the members of the Christian Church today. The pluralism of denominations provides variety, conflict, and confusion. With some of them making ethical issues out of morally neutral behavior, with others confusing what is possible ethically with the will of God for all people, and with others advocating actions and causes which are clearly unethical, the state of the Christian conscience is utterly confused.

Yet there are standards, as we made clear in the first portion

[4] See " 'Bobby-Sox' Religion," *Religious Education*, March–April, 1946, pp. 107–113.

of this chapter. We move from law to faith, and by God's grace we may know and do his will, knowing that we are creatures who are children of God. Exercises in ethical discrimination are of supreme importance, but it is easier to know God's will than to do it, and thus the whole of the Christian's faith in God is relevant to his behavior. His theological perspective and his membership in the Church with its channels of grace are part of the total picture. The learner needs not only to know what Christian ethics is, but also the power to do the same.

What we said about prayer as a source of power for the receiving of God's grace through faith needs to be correlated with Christian behavior. The old prayer, "Make me a good boy," is sound in its intention but vague in the application. "The soul's sincere desire" in a small boy needs to be concrete. "Help me to want to remember my piano lesson tomorrow" is relevant and opens the way for God to work through him. With an older group, the discussion of prayer and action might deal with a practical problem: your friend is sick in a hospital, so you may pray for him and forget about it, or you may go see him without praying at all and just barge into the sick room, or you may pray for him and for his doctors and nurses, and then go see him, telling him about the prayers, and perhaps bringing him some gift he would appreciate.

Well-rounded Christian nurture, provided by both home and Church, can do much to release the dynamic powers necessary for Christian living. Worship which is related to actual experiences of children may lead them through the basic psychological experiences of forgiveness and power and lead them to an understanding of their ethical dilemmas so that they may act to solve them.

A prayer simple enough for junior high age and up is the following:

"O Lord, we beseech thee mercifully to receive the prayers of thy people who call upon thee; and grant that they may both perceive and know what things they ought to do, and also may have grace and power faithfully to fulfil the same; through Jesus Christ our Lord. Amen." [5]

A prayer connected with preparation for confirmation is the following:

"Lord of all power and might, who art the author and giver of all good things; Graft in our hearts the love of thy Name, Increase in us true religion, Nourish us with all goodness, And of thy great mercy keep us in the same; through Jesus Christ our Lord. Amen." [6]

It is this relationship of prayer and action which is important, for one cannot divorce faith and works. Prayer is not completed without action or faith without works. The sources for this integration are found throughout the Christian tradition, in the Lord's Prayer, in the teachings of Jesus and especially in the Sermon on the Mount, in the interpretations of Jesus' teachings by Paul as he sought to make those teachings relevant to the newly converted communities to which he wrote his letters, in the stories of great persons throughout the history of the Church, in the men and women of today who seek to do their Father's will.

There is one final question which is often asked: "Why are so many good people outside the Church? Where do they get help, or do they need it?" There are many possible answers. Item number one is to ask, in return, "What happens in times of real crisis?" Reports from Germany tell us that the intellec-

[5] *The Book of Common Prayer*, p. 109.
[6] *Ibid.*, p. 283.

tuals who despised the Church were the first to sell out to Hitler, while those who believed most firmly in God held out the longest. Chaplains tell us that the soldiers who were active in their Christian worship held out longer against the temptations peculiar to soldiers. Those who have watched generations of actively Christian grandparents, nominally Christian parents, and unChristian children have reported a disintegration of moral calibre observable in the third generation, although the second generation seems to run on momentum. It has been said that it takes three generations to make, enjoy, and lose a fortune, and this is true whether one is banking money or drawing on the "bank of the saints." The insistence of law enforcement officers that full Sunday schools would mean empty jails may be an enthusiastic overstatement, but if the Sunday schools were as effective as they might be in connection with nurture in the home, there would be many great steps made toward a more Christian society.

Christians are not perfect even when they seem to have access to God's grace, but Christians are born with the same qualities as other men, and what marks off the true Christian is that his intentions are sound and his faith is sincere and his seeking to do God's will is without reservation. This does not automatically make him good, but it makes him a better follower of Jesus Christ than if he did not make this response to God's free offer of grace.

Arnold Toynbee, the great historian, has written, "It is obvious that for a number of generations we have been attempting to hold on to Christian practices without possessing Christian beliefs. But Christian behavior, which is not supported by Christian faith, is a wasting asset, as we have discovered to our great dismay."

Simple character guidance by itself, valuable as it may be, is not enough. "Goodness" is not enough. The Christian seeks to be "good for something" and "not good for nothing," and his goal is to "do good for God's sake." The obstacles of sin and ignorance with their cumulative effect in the workings of society leads away from Utopian dreams to a simple acceptance of the reign of God as the rule of life, and that should be enough for any man.

CHAPTER TEN
SOCIETY

THE thesis of all previous chapters has been that Christianity is relevant to all of life. As we have considered various theological doctrines, it has been in terms of the relevance of those doctrines for Christian living. If we believe that in Christianity there is the fundamental truth about God, about man and his relation to God, and about God's relation to man in the community of men, then our whole civilization must be measured in terms of Christian faith. Children need the background of this kind of perspective as surely as their parents.

The Church has always been concerned about the nature of society. It has never withdrawn from its social responsibilities, although there have been times when it lacked courage and conviction in the face of the challenges of society. The social imperative of Christian faith has taken different forms during the long history of the Church, and at times has seemed well-nigh forgotten, but the basic humanitarianism of the story of the Good Samaritan could never be neglected for long by those who considered themselves disciples of the Great Physician.[1]

[1] See William Temple, *Christianity and Social Order*, London: Student Christian Movement Press, for the best brief summary of this evidence.

I

For the thinking of American Christians today, the main background is provided by the "social gospel" of Walter Rauschenbusch and other prophets of the late nineteenth and early twentieth century. For awhile, the concern for a just social order overshadowed other aspects of Christian faith, and this overemphasis led to a distortion of theology, especially as regards the doctrine of man. The natural swing of the pendulum following the discrediting of the optimistic view of man's nature led to a discrediting of some elements in the social gospel, and in some cases the swing went so far as to deny the social value of Christian faith.

There are certain new factors in our knowledge of man and society which indicate that the social relevance of Christianity is as important in evaluating the purpose of the Church as the Church's other functions. Modern sociological research has made it clear that environment is one of the greatest of all the conditioning factors in the development of personality. While it is possible for a mature soul to gain some degree of independence from his environment, our knowledge of child psychology shows how much the conditioning process of the home determines the direction of growth of the persons in a home. Poor food, unsanitary conditions, overcrowded shacks, racial pressures, parental discord, absence of one parent due to employment or war, unemployment, lack of money to buy children the little things that enrich their leisure, the impact of totalitarian political pressures on the parents and children, and other social factors have a direct effect upon the development of Christian character.

This sociological consideration affects the Church's social strategy from two points of view. From the standpoint of evangelism, it is the hope of the Church that men may have an opportunity to be drawn to Christ and to become his obedient servants. When the external conditions are so extreme that a man must be concerned with the satisfying of his minimum physical wants, there is not much opportunity for the Gospel of Christ to speak to him, except perhaps as a needed opiate. When all the conditionings of his character point in a direction foreign to the commandments of God, there is little chance to develop in him a sense of the will of God as righteousness and love. So the Church becomes a champion of social reform because such reform is a precondition to the evangelistic work which the Church is called by God to perform.

The Church's interest in social reform is also dictated by its concern for persons. The cure of souls is not just an individual matter when one observes the debilitating effects of unemployment. It is not only suffering and privation which arouse Christian sympathy, important as this is in all the Church's work in hospitals and social work, but it is the effect upon the personalities of those who are crushed by the oppressions of an unjust social system. These are simple sociological insights which have been clarified by scientific research but which have been part of the Gospel since the first time the story of the Good Samaritan was told.

A second major factor in determining the Church's social strategy for today is recognition of the existence of social change. The changes are going to take place, for better or for worse, in terms of evolution and revolution, with justice in some cases and injustice in others. There is no plateau of realized social progress upon which any civilization can rest, and a culture will either move upward or it will fall to a lower level. While the Church has often identified itself with the *status quo* in times past, frequently because the State was wise enough to take unto itself the blessing of the Church and the doctrine of the divine right of kings or dictators, the more recent devel-

opments of Christian thinking have made clear the right of
oppressed people to conduct a revolution. This has been a
predominant thought in American Christianity which was
given its greatest stimulus to growth as a result of the American War of Independence. Whether the Church likes it or
not, these social changes are taking place, and in many theologies which reflect the social righteousness of the Hebrew
prophets there is a basis for this revolutionary way of thinking
in the doctrine of God. A sound Jewish-Christian theology,
which is sufficiently Biblical and sufficiently freed from
European feudalism and its hangovers, takes revolution as
part of God's purpose in history.

The changes in modern society offer great opportunities
for both injustice and justice in the new forms of culture. The
increasing weakness of the Church as far as political attach-
ments are concerned gives it greater freedom to make use of
its prophetic function as the conscience of the State. If the
Church comes to a full realization of the importance of the
changes taking place, of the opportunities for new kinds of
justice among new areas and classes of people, and of the stake
which the Church has as an institution in these processes of
change, there must be a strategy among the Churches which
will encourage the achievement of Christian ideals and Christian purposes in the newer forms of society.

Another element in the changed sociological climate which
the weather men of the Church must see and predict clearly
is the rise in social and political power of various minority
groups. These groups are formed on economic, political, and
racial lines. They have not been incorporated into the life of
the Churches, which continue to represent primarily the
outlook of bourgeois people and standards. The labor unions
operate independently of the Christian institutions, although
the concern of the Churches for labor has sometimes aroused
labor's interest. The conspicuous failure of the Churches to

live up to their claims to equality in the area of race relations, plus the acquiescence of the Churches in the colonial expansion of great empires, has indicated that the Churches may not fare too well in the changes in society which will mark the rise of oppressed racial groups to positions of power. It has been suggested that one of the chief reasons for the rise of Communism has been the failure of Christianity to meet the needs of the oppressed classes; that is why we can say that "Communism as a faith and as a system of thought is a compound of half-truth and positive error," [2] in which the half-truths offer serious criticisms of Christianity, but in which the positive suggestions for the cure of humanity's evils are so full of error that Christians must resist any Communist expansion in the world.

Other elements in the environment are causing changes in the social outlook of the Churches. The industrial culture in which we live, with all the advantages of a machine age, provides an orientation new to this generation. The products of the machine age, unknown in the past century, have become indispensable to comfortable living. The machine has become a focal point in the process of living. The human mind is formed by what it uses, what it is concerned with, what it dreams about. He that looks on a machine with lust in his heart is already guilty of covetousness. Our security becomes other than the grace of God when we are secure in our possessions. Our gadgets have become so complex that we are helpless when they break down until an expert is called in. We have become more dependent on the plumber than we are on God. Our country is no longer God's country but a plumber's paradise.

Because of this concern for machines, social power also

[2] John C. Bennett, *Christianity and Communism.* New York: Association Press (Haddam House), p. 9. Cf. his *Christian Ethics and Social Policy,* pp. 1–14, on "The Christian Social Imperative."

becomes mechanized. The only test of a job-holder or of his boss is, Can he produce? The depersonalizing forces of the mechanized world are such that personal qualities are completely overlooked. Even the conflict between labor and capital is between impersonal organizations and is not solved in the crucible of truly personal relationships.

All of these changes in modern society, where various new "isms" compete for the loyalties of men are not new in their fundamental nature. There is a "new comparative religion" only in the sense that modern developments have provided new live options, such as Marxism, nationalistic mysticism, scientism, secular humanism, the faith of labor, and other forms of nonChristian options. We have substituted atomic bombs for swords, radio for grapevine, secularism for old Christian heresies, and the evil is the same: the pride and greed and lust of men.[3]

The Church stands as a witness against all depersonalizing forces in modern civilization, not by aligning itself with entrenched privilege and the *status quo* and not by identifying itself with a particular solution to the problem. The first act of the Church in witnessing against the subjugation of man to any man-made power or machine is worship. This is the primary function of the Church. When the body of believers worships God, there are no automatons. Each worshiper is a *person*, a creature of Almighty God. The power which comes from worship is personalized power which is the gift of a gracious God. The one upon whom the grace of God has fallen knows himself as a person, because his relationship with God is personal.

It is in the Church that the worshiper knows himself to be a worshiper of "mammon," which symbolizes money, power, prestige, and things, and he admits that this is wrong, and that

[3] See articles in *The Church and Organized Movements* by Elton Trueblood and Bishop Edward L. Parsons, New York: Harper, esp. pp. 33-42, 235.

he must love people more than things. This does not solve his external relations in a depersonalized society of power politics, but it makes him a man as he faces society's challenge.

The Church is a worshiping fellowship, and every member of that community knows that every other member is a person in the sight of God, regardless of any distinctions which may mar his citizenship among pagan men.

The first witness of the Church is its worship. The very language of worship is a protest against all kinds of injustice. A few phrases from the classic prayers of Christendom make this clear: "Whose service is perfect freedom. . . . Defend our liberties and fashion into one united people the multitudes brought hither out of many kindreds and tongues. . . . Take away all hatred and prejudice, and whatever else may hinder us from godly union and concord. . . . Grant us grace fearlessly to contend against evil, and to make no peace with oppression. . . . Incline the heart of employers and of those whom they employ to mutual forbearance, fairness, and good will. . . . Guide the nations of the world into the way of justice and truth, and establish among them that peace which is the fruit of righteousness, that they may become the Kingdom of our Lord and Saviour Jesus Christ."

The Church's domain in both worship and action is the whole world of human experience. Its main job is not ethical or social legislation, but in its place as the central institution of the Christian religion, one of the chief concerns of the Church is the formulating of ethical ideals which are approximations of the will of God for specific situations. In stating these ideals, the Church hopes to inspire social legislation, to influence leaders among statesmen, to encourage citizens to support good leaders and good laws, and to stimulate actions which will bring about conditions which are closer to God's will for the world.

It is proper for the Church to make statements concerning child labor, planned parenthood, liquor conditions, race problems, industrial relations, slave labor camps, denials of religious freedom, war, and peace; but its main task is not to dictate legislation. It uses its persuasiveness, working through its Christian members, to bring about the elimination of social and ethical evils and to make possible the increase of that which is good. The Church by itself may never stop war, but it can and does inspire men to work for peace and international cooperation. While a revised United Nations may be necessary to set up the machinery of peace, the World Council of Churches will do more to inspire it.

While the Church has no business legislating about major or minor matters, and should make only the most general provisions for its members, it should still be deeply concerned with the personal and social ethics of its environment. Such statements as the official pronouncements of denominational leaders, the occasional findings of the Federal Council of Churches, and the report of such ecumenical conferences as Oxford and Amsterdam on matters of personal and social ethics, carry with them a profound and guiding authority. These statements are a basis for the preaching and witness of all the Churches, and thus they are worked into the minds of individual members of the Churches.

If the Church should enter directly into politics, it would cease to be a persuasive and inspiring force. This would turn it into a political power, and it might be as effective as the Roman Church frequently has been. When a Church failed or was proved wrong (as has been the case at times), it would lose prestige and thus lessen its future persuasive and inspiring force. When it succeeded, it would become a slave of the power it had used, and thus would serve other ends than the will of God, as is abundantly evident in the record of Vatican politics. Furthermore, only a totalitarian Church may afford the luxury of unanimity on any social or ethical problem.

Individual Christians (even ministers), simply because their authority is less, have the right to be more direct and demanding than the Church in seeking social change. The Church might support prohibition in principle, but individual Christians, *as Christians*, could demand a certain type of legislation to control the obvious evils of freely flowing liquors. The Church may make statements concerning the justice of a particular war, and still allow freedom among individual members to choose between participation and conscientious objection. On many issues, Christians and even Churches may differ, as in the case of child labor, and each group will feel bound to support opposite sides. This does not mean that God's will is divided, but that men, as usual, have an inadequate or partial grasp of his will.

The problem of Christian ethics is the discovery of God's will and doing it. The discovery is difficult in itself. We need to call forth all our resources—of reason, observation, imagination, will, and love—in order to have even an approximation in our mind, and then we need to call forth all our energy, sense of direction, and faith in order to achieve even the approximation we have sensed. It is no wonder that ethical idealism fails; it is not surprising that so many Christians fail; for without the strength that comes only from the grace of God, no man can achieve the will of God for him, and then he will fall into sin again and again. The sin of pride will come from achievement and spoil what God's grace has made possible, or he will fail in his intention and sin from the beginning. In either case, God's forgiveness must be part of his grace if we are to have any sanity at all in the world. The Christian is a citizen of two worlds, and the tensions between these worlds are never completely resolved. But both worlds are bearable because God is equally present and sovereign in both, and man is always a son of God as well as a sinner—in the sight of both worlds and of God.[4]

Theologically, this interpretation of Christian ethics is based upon the kingdom of God. The kingdom has meant many things in the history of theology, but primarily it means the reign or sovereignty of God, and geographical and chronological question are secondary. The kingdom, wherever and whenever it should come, represented a religious hope of social redemption. It was based upon the religion of the prophets. It would come as a result of an act of God.

It is true that the New Testament represents the kingdom as an event which would come in the near future or as already here. Both the Gospels and Paul's letters are full of this hope and expectation. It is also true that some early Christians conceived of the fall of Jerusalem as the event which fulfilled the prophecies of Jesus and Paul, while other Christians have related it to Pentecost and have found the kingdom in the Church. Alfred Loisy put it succinctly when he wrote, "What Jesus announced was the kingdom of God; what came was the Catholic Church." [5] But the Church never became more than a community in the quest of the kingdom.

The clue to the meaning of the kingdom when all other problems are swept away is found in two phrases from the Lord's Prayer: "Thy kingdom come, thy will be done on earth as it is in heaven," and the ascription added to Matthew's original account, "Thine is the kingdom, and the power, and the glory forever." The idea of the kingdom begins with God as sovereign, as in complete control of all the processes of nature and of history. The kingdom is the heart of Christian living, for it is beyond any human ideal and thus is a concept wide enough to symbolize what God's will may be.

[4] See my article "The Relevance of Christian Ethics," *Religion in Life*, XIV:2, pp. 214–215.
[5] Quoted by F. C. Grant, *Anglican Theological Review*, XXI, p. 191.

The sovereign Lord of history is God of the moral law. The idea of the day of judgment is tied in with the kingdom, and Amos prophesied that the day of Yahweh would be a day of doom. The symbolism of the coming kingdom with its message, "The time is fulfilled, and the kingdom of God is at hand: repent, and believe in the gospel" (Mk. 1:15, A), and the symbolism of the second coming of Christ point to the same fact of experience: that God is a righteous and moral God of judgment.

On the negative side of judgment, and on the positive side of submission to the Kingship of God, the idea of the kingdom is essentially ethical. It is recognition of the complete sovereignty of a moral God. As far as men are concerned, we say that the kingdom is present wherever God's will is done, and this is the requirement as seen in the Lord's Prayer; but "God is not mocked," and he remains the king of all creation even when he is disobeyed. If God's will were done on earth as it is in heaven, his kingdom would be present among men; and if God's will were done universally, his reign would be complete and the kingdom would have come fully.

The relevance of the idea of the kingdom of God becomes clear even in this brief treatment. God wills that men should live together in brotherhood; God values all men equally and loves them so much that he sent his only begotten Son to save them. The Church, which is the community of the faithful in quest of God's kingdom, seeks to bring about those conditions whereby God will act to bring in his kingdom. This concept provides a guide for men's ethical and social behavior, and thus Christian ethics, as grounded in the religious dimension, is relevant to every activity of every man. The kingdom is thus within the hearts of those who are absolutely committed to God's will, and the kingdom stands beyond history, for God's will is done in heaven as it should be done in earth. The kingdom is the goal of all human endeavor and stands in judg-

ment upon all human effort, and only by repentance and faith
may men enter God's kingdom by his grace.

In a paraphrase from the eucharistic prayer of the *Didache*,
written about 110 A.D., there is this stanza:

> "Watch o'er thy Church, O Lord, in mercy,
> Save it from evil, guard it still,
> Perfect it in thy love, unite it,
> Cleansed and conformed unto thy will.
> As grain, once scatter'd on the hillsides,
> Was in this broken bread made one,
> So from all lands thy Church be gathered
> Into thy kingdom by thy Son" [6]

II

Real concern for the sufferings and tragedies of others is not
a quality of childhood sympathy except as it concerns individuals. They can react to the personalized suffering of the
travelling Jew in the story of the Good Samaritan, but they
can hardly get excited or comprehend the meaning of the
death of millions of Jews under Hitler. Their social problem is acute enough in terms of adaptation to their own
community.

As a result, smaller children are excited about a visit to the
firehouse, or a study of neighborhood helpers who come within
their range of experience, such as the milkman and the garbage
man. They may be concerned with the injustices of the playground, but only in terms of particular instances, for they
have the problem of learning how to get along with other
children who have been differently conditioned in their
reactions.

Their ethical growth is primarily personal, and not particu-

[6] *The Hymnal*, 1940, No. 195. Tr. by F. Bland Tucker.

larly related to the will of God. Indeed, there is danger at this point of associating the presence of God with a celestial policeman if too much emphasis is placed upon God's concern with their actions. The theological concept of the kingdom of God is irrelevant to their strivings to achieve basic patterns of behavior response which will please their parents and teachers and enable them to get along with the members of their experienced community.

The junior can take a step forward. He has had enough experiences to be aware of the widespread injustice and the various social problems of his entire community, which is probably a cross-section of America. He knows about people who are out of work, he knows what it means to be on relief, a friend's father may be out on strike, he sees the segregation of Negroes, he hears nasty remarks about Jews, his own mother may have to work, he may live in a congested neighborhood or know those who do, he has seen enough motion pictures to be aware of crime, of having servants in a home, and of those who go hungry. He has heard talk around the table at home about war, about Communism, and about the liquor problem.

One of the most brilliant courses for fifth and sixth graders is Edna Baxter's *Living and Working in Our Country*, which deals with problems of hunger and relief, labor, coal miners, unions and strikes, child labor and migrant workers, workers in cotton, co-operatives, housing, and dealing with various racial groups. A great deal of this material is good social science, but throughout the course it is related to worship, with prayers, litanies, and hymns. Among the hymns for juniors are suggested Whittier's "O brother man, fold to thy heart thy brother," Merrill's "Rise up, O men of God," North's "Where cross the crowded ways of life," and "America, the beautiful." An ethical imperative grows out of this course, but the full implications of social ethics and theology are still too difficult.

Another approach to this problem on the fifth grade level is the study of Jewish customs, as in Dorothy LeCroix Hill's *The Way of Good Will*. A comparative study of worship among Jews, Roman Catholics, and Protestants is enticingly presented to this age group in Florence Mary Fitch's *One God*.

In all age groups from the junior through high school, effective courses on social ethics are available. On the high school level, it is possible to relate the social gospel to theology. Harold Hunting has done this in two courses, *Your World and How to Live in It* and *Thy Kingdom Come*. Against the background of what Jesus meant by the kingdom of God, the problems of modern society are faced squarely. At the end of the course is the question, "What would our community be like if the kingdom of God should begin to come? Our homes? Our country? Our world?" A thorough-going discussion based upon Christian presuppositions, dealing with what the Church should do and what individual Christians should do in facing social problems, is fitted into this framework. Going back to Wilberforce and the abolition of slavery, telling the story of Susan B. Anthony and the liberation of women, recalling the rise of the social gospel in England and America, and then looking at such modern problems as war and the United Nations, the interpretation of "daily bread" in terms of poverty, collective bargaining, Karl Marx, co-operatives, and the profit motive, at racial distinctions and segregation, at family life in the twentieth century, at the handling of criminals, at the use of alcohol, at the use of leisure, and at the conflict between science and religion, the course concludes with consideration of the unique mission of the Church in relation to all human predicaments of this kind.

Possibly the most hopeful sign among the new generation of Christians is that they are not illiterate about the social gospel. Lesson materials written from the standpoint of progressive educational philosophy have always contained a good deal of social ethics, although few of them have been integrated theologically as successfully as Dr. Hunting's units.

The worship of our Church schools has assisted this development. The twentieth century hymns have a note of social action lacking in such old time favorites as "Nearer, my God, to thee." John Oxenham's great "In Christ there is no East or West" is sung in most Church schools today, and where the tune is by Burleigh the poignancy of the words is fully brought out. Richards' "Our Father, thy dear Name doth show the greatness of thy love," is another popular favorite. Not so well known, but appealing to activistic juniors as well as to adults, is Russell's hymn, the opening stanza of which is,

> "Christian, rise, and act thy creed,
> Let thy prayer be in thy deed;
> Seek the right, perform the true,
> Raise thy work and life anew." [7]

Van Dyke's "Jesus, thou divine Companion" and Oxenham's "All labor gained new dignity" stresses the importance of work. The third stanza of Bowie's "Lord Christ, when first thou cam'st to men," gives meaning through worship to the idea of judgment for social unrighteousness and relates it to the kingdom:

> "New advent of the love of Christ,
> Shall we again refuse thee,
> Till in the night of hate and war
> We perish as we lose thee?
> From old unfaith our souls release
> To seek the kingdom of thy peace,
> By which alone we choose thee." [8]

Many modern hymns, it may easily be seen, show the relationship between theology and social ethics in language which the

[7] *Christian Praise and Worship*, No. 483.
[8] *The Hymnal*, 1940, No. 522.

high school age may understand. Perhaps the continuing prayer for this approach to Christian living might be Harry Emerson Fosdick's refrain,

> "Grant us wisdom, grant us courage,
> Lest we miss thy kingdom's goal." [9]

The life of fellowship and worship within the Church is the great powerhouse of action by persons to bring God's will to fulfillment. The rhythm of worship is such that it includes clearing away all obstacles, listening to what God's will may be, and then through prayer gaining power to do his will. "Repent, for the kingdom of God is at hand," has an added urgency when modern forms of technology shorten the time available for repentance. Christian education needs to move forward now with the cry of "prepare ye the way of the Lord."

[9] *Christian Worship and Praise*, No. 464, stanza 3. *The Hymnal*, 1940, No. 524.

CHAPTER ELEVEN
AUTHORITY

I

THE basic source book of Christian theology is the Bible. It is accepted as the record of the mighty acts of God in history, whereby he revealed himself to men. Our concern for theology as the background for all Christian education, with the relationship between God and man at the center of that process, brings to the fore the question of the authority of the Bible and the degree of freedom which men should have in interpreting their own faith as members of the Christian community. Both children and parents are often confused about their approach to the authority of the Bible and its relevance in the twentieth century.

It is the thesis of this book that the source of all authority and all freedom is God, who has revealed himself to men in events of history and in nature. The primary seat of revelation and thus of authority is found in the Bible as interpreted by the concept of "the mind of Christ." All other authorities, such as the Church, the creeds, the ministry or the episcopate, reason, and conscience, are inferior to the authority of Holy Scripture.

There are two levels of freedom which are essential to this understanding of the place of authority. The first is the simple freedom which is necessary in order to submit to any authority, so that beliefs however acquired may be the basis of faith which demands an act of the will. In other words, one has freedom to submit to Rome, to a fundamentalist interpretation of the Bible, to the Inner Light, to a particular denominational tradition, or to a liberal interpretation of Christianity. The second kind of freedom is what remains after one has selected his authority, and this freedom varies with the denominations, or with the traditions within a denomination, or within the general point of view of American Protestantism. Both authority and freedom are correlated for us under the concept of loyalty to the God revealed through Jesus Christ and to the Church which is the Body of Christ.

Authority in religion is simply rightful power. It is not coercive power, but rather partakes of the nature of moral persuasion, which is both trustworthy and living in its hold upon men who admit such authority. To be an authority in this sense, it must be immediately recognizable as such. Jesus taught "as one *having* authority" and not as one who taught *from* authority. It is something offered and accepted as truth. There is, then, no distinction between religions of authority and of the spirit, for where there is authority the Spirit of God is active. The authority of the Christian revelation rests in God's word, which is the power of redemption. God is the source of authority, and it is our problem to find the seat of authority.[1]

To have freedom is to be independent of an arbitrary, external power. It is exemption from necessity in thought or action. It is the right to use one's reason and come to one's own conclusions. It is freedom to believe or not to believe, to

[1] See W. Norman Pittenger, *His Body the Church*, p. 110; Vergilius Ferm, ed., *Encyclopedia of Religion*, p. 48; also, "Authority and Freedom in Doctrine," in Theodore Ferris, ed., *Episcopalians United*; *My Religion Makes Sense*, pp. 219–227.

accept or not to accept, to interpret in one way or another any given doctrine.

If this distinction between religious authority and freedom is correct, it follows that authority operates through the sense of obligation, being moral persuasion. Obligation is meaningless unless one can select his response to an "ought" or an "ought not." Thus, authority presupposes freedom as basic to its existence.

While there were many different interpretations of the seat of authority at the time of the Reformation, there was complete agreement that "Holy Scripture containeth all things necessary to salvation." The words "contain" and "necessary" are important, for this means that *within* the Bible is to be found a unique, true, final, and saving revelation of the one true God: that is the indisputable claim made by all Protestant Christians. The Bible contains, that is, has within it, all that is necessary for man to be saved. The Bible in its wholeness gives us the story of the revelation of God culminating in the historical events of the life, death, and resurrection of Jesus Christ, which we have summarized in the doctrines of the Incarnation and Atonement.

This is, of course, a very general authority except that it gives us a center from which to estimate its nature. "The duty and authority of the Church to preach the Gospel derive from Christ, and from no other source. If we are asked 'by what authority?' we can only answer—in the last analysis—'In the Name of Jesus.' " [2] We come to "the mind of Christ" as the perspective by which we evaluate the authority of Scripture, and this view lacks the clarity of legal and literal renderings of authority, but "the Christian conception of the Word must reject theories that mechanize the Word and fail to see that the Word appears in the form of a human witness, as well as

[2] Lesslie Newbigin, in *The Church's Witness to God's Design. Amsterdam Assembly Series.* New York: Harpers, Vol. II, p. 20.

theories according to which the character of the divine message appears in a spirtualized way. The Spirit speaks in and through the Word. Only in this way is the Spirit given." [3]

All other authorities are inferior to that of Scripture, although the Church reserves the right to make decisions in controversies of faith, provided it remains subject to the Word of God. The creeds of the Church are valuable as summaries of doctrine, but they are statements of faith rather than belief. The creeds may be accepted in a symbolic sense. In the Church of England, for example, where creeds are used in every service, there is this point of view: Statements in the creed which cannot be accepted literally may "have value as pictorial statements of spiritual truths, even though the supposed facts themselves did not actually happen. . . . It is not therefore illegitimate to accept and affirm particular clauses in the creeds in this symbolic fashion," but this must be qualified with a limitation. "It is, however, in any case essential to hold that the facts underlying the Gospel story—which story the creeds summarize and interpret—were such as to justify the Gospel itself." [4] The ministry of the Church, especially among those communions which have bishops, is authoritative in the sense that helpful leadership is given in the interpretation of the basic authority of Scripture, and rulings in terms of discipline may be provided to enforce certain interpretations, but always in theory such decisions are in terms of submission to the authority of Scripture itself. The annual or other regular meetings of the constituted representatives of the members of any denomination also have a legislative authority which is quite sweeping, but all such activity is subsumed under the authority of the Bible. The same thing is true of the ecumenical conferences and statements.

[3] Gustaf Aulén, *The Universal Church and God's Design. Amsterdam Assembly Series.* New York: Harpers, Vol. I, p. 23.
[4] *Doctrine in the Church of England.* New York: Macmillan, pp. 37–38.

Authority is from God (as freedom is from God). The authority of all finite things and persons depends upon the degree to which they reveal the Source. If God is acting through this medium, there is authority. The devil can cite Scripture, majority rule can upset a council, the Church can be corrupted by a Pope or clerical hierarchy, and creeds can crystallize belief and paralyze faith. We have a Gospel, which is the good news of God in Jesus Christ, but we can turn it into empty ceremonial, superstitious belief, and bibliolatry. Only when authority is correlated with freedom, when authority is self-validating because its truth can be demonstrated, when the Bible and traditions and creeds portray and reveal the living God in Christ, is there Christian authority.

The individual *in the Church*, therefore, retains freedom and the right of private judgment. Authority may command belief, but faith involves personal appropriation. The individual should know which beliefs he accepts on authority and which he has made part of his personal faith through experience. Professor Edward S. Drown used to say that "no doctrine is a Christian doctrine which does not spring from the experience of God in Christ and does not apply to the Christian life." [5] Experience in the corporate, historic, and worshiping sense is essential to the verification of all truth.

Experience by individuals is not enough. Whether it be the dramatic experience of Paul, the sense of forgiveness of the penitent, or the calm resourcefulness of consistent devotion, experience as a single court of appeal is open to charges of subjectivism, undue privacy, and contradictory interpretations. It is not without reason that the Church has been suspicious of its mystics and quietists, even though it respects the doctrine of the Inner Light as the work of the Holy Spirit and holds to the right of private judgment. History and reason

[5] Quoted by J. A. Muller, *The Episcopal Theological School: 1867–1943.* Cambridge: Episcopal Theological School, p. 205.

must be brought to bear upon the interpretation of both individual and corporate experience before its validity can be proclaimed.

Without experience, however, all authority is external. When a belief is translated into faith through the gracious personal act of the living God, there is freedom to accept or reject what has been received from an authoritative Christian community. It is at this point that freedom enters the picture.

This freedom exists for two reasons. The first is to make room for honest difference of opinion, so that members of the Churches may say to each other, "in things essential, unity; in things doubtful, liberty; in all things, charity." But the second reason is more profound, for it is the recognition that freedom is essential for the discovery of God's truth. Too often the Church has obstructed the search for truth and thus has hindered God's revelation of himself. The acceptance of the findings of Biblical scholarship, for example, has changed radically the attitude toward Scripture without distorting or destroying its authority. The advances in the sciences have given new insight into the Church's work in many fields and enriched the interpretation of the Church's theology. The Church of today is aware of Erasmus' warning, "By identifying the new learning with heresy, you make orthodoxy synonymous with ignorance."

Both freedom and authority are subsumed under the concept of loyalty to the living God and to the Christian community. Where there is loyalty within the Church and to the Church, there is a common "catholic" nucleus which has moral authority without compromising the freedom of its individual members. Where there is loyalty to the God revealed in Jesus Christ, a consecrated reason may safely examine the inherited doctrines of the Church and the historical foundations of the basis for loyalty. Where there is loyalty to God's will in the working out of problems, God's revelation may be given through the activity of his Holy Spirit. Thus authority and freedom are blended together in the worshiping community which has its roots in an historical revelation. These irrevocable historical events are an inescapable primary datum for any theology. As loyal members of the Body of Christ, we freely accept his Lordship and seek by all the tools he has given us to find the truth.

II

The Bible is relevant to the experiences of children and adults, although in quite different ways as far as the presentation of material is concerned. What we have provided in the preceding pages of this chapter is a theological interpretation of the Bible as a basis for Christian faith on the adult level, and we have thereby implied that the theology in the other chapters of this book is based upon the interpretation of the authority of the Bible as summarized.

The Bible, then, is the primary source book for Christian faith, and it is important to know the Bible theologically. How often have children been exposed to Bible "stories" in Church school, with no perspective for knowing why such incidents were being related. Just as we have taught the life of Jesus the "good man" with no framework of the faith in Jesus as the Christ, so we have taught the Bible as interesting history about some Jewish peasants and heroes, or as a book of infallible doctrine.

The way in which the Bible should be taught, and all Christian literature should be taught, is described by Adelaide Case: "Christian education is the effort to make available for our generation—children, young people, and adults—the accumulated treasures of Christian life and thought, in such a way that God in Christ may carry on His redemptive work in each human soul and in the common life of man." [6]

When we turn to the various age-groups, it is surprising how little of the Bible we can use. The pre-school child often suffers through many Bible stories, but they have no educational value at all. Possibly two or three New Testament *incidents*, tied in with the showing of a suitable picture, is as much as we can hope for with the three year old. These brief explanations should be repeated frequently. Perhaps the love of a mother for her baby, familiar enough experiences to the child, may be used as part of the Christmas season, and the baby may even be named "Jesus." We need to remember that the story of Jesus and the children is effective teaching with older children and adults, and this means being careful not to dull its edge by introducing it too early.

In order to present a childhood Bible experience, some teachers distort stories which have a child appearing in them, thus not teaching the religion of the Bible at all. Presentations of Samuel and David often suffer from such misrepresentation. It is better to avoid such stories until they may be taught from a Christian point of view.

Kindergarten children, having reached five years of age, will listen to stories of about five hundred words. Vocabulary, scenery, and events must still be limited to their experiences and imaginations. The picture drawn of kinds of life in the Bible must not be too different from what they know. But above all, the religious teaching must be sound. Unless the Old Testament stories are evaluated in terms of the concept of God in the New Testament, there is danger of damage to the developing theology of the kindergarten children. The best approach is through the constant and creative use of New

[6] Quoted by Dora Chaplin, *Children and Religion*. New York: Scribners, p. 136.

Testament stories especially suited to this age. A favorable at-titude toward the Bible, toward Jesus, and toward the leading characters is more important than any memorizing of pas-sages.

The only test of Biblical material at any age is whether it leads to increased faith in God and growing fellowship with other children and adults. The Bible is a tool of Christian living, not a text book to be assimilated. The kindergarten teacher will have a store of applicable Bible stories to use when the life situation of the learners calls for them, and there-fore the Bible will speak to the nurture of the children. Occa-sionally, stories from the Bible may be given in the language of one of the English translations, including of course the King James, Revised Standard, Goodspeed, and Moffatt, but more often with these younger children the stories will be told in their own language. One of the better examples of books which may be read and shown to kindergarten (and primary) children is Pelagie Doane's *A Small Child's Bible* (Oxford), although most teachers would prefer to select even from this fine collection, for some of them meet the adult demand for stories rather than the children's need for God.

Concerning memory, it may be said simply that memorizing for the purpose of corporate worship, when the material has classic value as well, is justified even when it is not under-stood, provided it is used constantly. Memorizing for the sake of retention of ideas before the age of nine is a complete waste of time, especially the Bible verses which are simply a drill.

A few more Bible stories, up to about one thousand words in length, are available for first and second grade children, but the same principles apply as in the case of the five year olds. They are now going to public or private elementary schools, but they still have not mastered the techniques of reading sufficiently for effective Christian teaching. More use may be made of the Bible itself, and comparisons of various translations are possible. Bible stories often can be paralleled by modern incidents, and frequently the children will provide a similar experience of their own.

While there is no historical sense in primary children, they can understand something of Biblical backgrounds, but above all they can begin to see that the chief character in the Bible is God, that Jesus Christ stands out as the chief figure in what God does, and that the Bible helps us to understand God and Jesus. The constant use of the Bible in worship gives it meanings which are valuable to the growing child. To begin a service of worship with such phrases as the following builds up sound attitudes: "I was glad when they said unto me, We will go into the house of the Lord" (Psalm 122:1,PB), "This is the day which the Lord hath made; we will rejoice and be glad in it" (Psalm 118:24,PB).

The third grade child is able to read, and should be classed with the juniors for Bible teaching. The Bible is now a tool for research, to be used in connection with workbooks, posters, dramatic skits, and whatever else the imaginative teacher discovers to be of interest and value to the boys and girls. Bible stories of a more dramatic and vivid kind may be used. Memory work is worth while when it is selected for a reason clear to the juniors. More background material can be provided, thus giving new meanings to the references to shepherds of Israel in the "I am the good shepherd" of the Fourth Gospel or the twenty-third psalm. A remarkable selection of stories which appeal to juniors is Edgar J. Goodspeed's *The Junior Bible*, and there are many others in various translations which appear each year. Because of the price, it is hard to find Bibles to give to juniors, but the best print and most accurate translation is the *Revised Standard Version*, although it has no illustrations. The cheapest book of selections for this age is the Modern Library edition of the Goodspeed *Short Bible*, which has the value of providing excellent historical introductions.[7]

By the sixth grade, the historical sense is well developed, and many ways of approach suggest themselves as we look at the characteristics of twelve year olds. The theory of Christian education expounded in these chapters is best illustrated in the courses available at this and the intermediate level. It is here that Biblical scholarship may be used, the reason the books were written may be studied, and the background of the specific teachings may be grasped. Dora Chaplin suggests that the best approach is through this material and also through the story of the printing and translations of the Bible.[8]

One of the finest approaches to the New Testament for junior high boys and girls is *The New Testament and You,* by Mary White.[9] It makes full use of the findings of Biblical scholarship, never loses sight of the theological and ethical relevance of the New Testament to the experiences of intermediate boys and girls, and presents Jesus Christ as the central figure. It begins with Paul's letters, makes use of Goodspeed's theory of how Paul's letters were saved and edited, and then relates the central themes of these letters to such experiences as "The surprise element," "Can you keep your mind made up?" "Is freedom all fun?" "What difference does God make?" "Do you believe all you hear?" Each of the Gospels is approached from the question of why the book was written, and then come the questions, "What is Jesus like?" "What is the kingdom of heaven?" "How shall we start?" Then comes the story of the early Church as found in Acts and the later Epistles. A fascinating approach to the letter of James under

[7] Ethel Smither, *The Use of the Bible with Children.* Nashville: Abingdon-Cokesbury, is the best treatment of this subject for children from nursery through the first six grades.

[8] *Children and Religion,* pp. 104–137.

[9] New York: Morehouse-Gorham (Cloister Series).

the title, "What makes a sermon good?" leads into a study of character and worship. Theology stands behind this course, historical study dictates the order of approach, the psychology of the boys and girls determines the method. It is theological, factual, honest, and life-centered.

There are other courses for this age level which do the same things for both the Old and New Testaments, and some of them may also be used for high school students who are having similar experiences. The subtitles of one course are fascinating: Abraham: "Must you do as the crowd does?" Jacob: "Do you know the green worm of jealousy?" Moses: "How do you get over an inferiority complex?" David: "Does popularity pay?" [10] A study of the prophets leads to both faith in God and the demand for social righteousness. The psalms become the basis for studying the place of hymns in worship.

On the high school level, an entirely new approach to the Bible may be used. It is here that the question of authority comes to the fore. If the teacher has been intelligent in handling Biblical stories as myths, legends, drama, poetry, and history in the earlier grades, no conflicts of any importance will arise until the skepticism of the high school mind is turned on the problem of authority. A high school class, using the discussion method, could begin with the thesis that the Bible is the story of how God made himself known to the people of Israel and to all people since then. The central figure is God, who is the person to look for behind every story, poem, law, parable, drama, and historical fact. Because Christianity is an historical religion, we can expect the Bible to have its ups and downs, and it is good to note some unethical acts of Yahweh in the Old Testament for perspective. If we understand that the Bible is *religious* literature, rather

[10] *The Old Testament and You.* New York: Morehouse-Gorham.

than scientific or Elizabethan in its nature, we can see that it records mighty acts of God which culminate in Christ. At this point, the study of the Bible is correlated with all that we have said about the place of theology in Christian education, and the authority of the Bible is centered in "the mind of Christ." The Bible tells us what people thought about Christ, and this brings us back to the focal point of our religious living, which is faith in Jesus Christ as Lord and Savior. The relation of authority and freedom in religious thinking could be worked out by a check list such as the following:

"No Church, no clergyman, no friend, no book can *make* you believe anything. You have to believe for yourself. How would you rate the following tests for your belief in Christ?

a. It is found in the Old Testament.
b. It makes sense; it checks with my experience.
c. My parents told me.
d. Jesus said it.
e. The minister said it was true.
f. St. Paul wrote it.
g. I feel convinced, deep-down-inside, that it has to be true.
h. I want to believe it, even if there is no evidence, because it makes me feel better." [11]

When these questions were asked of one class, both at the beginning and at the end of a year's study, there was great variation in the answers. The problem of religious authority was being faced and worked out in the crucible of discussion and the comparing of experiences.

It is a far cry from the nursery incident to the high school

[11] See my *The Challenge of the Church*, New York: Morehouse-Gorham, student's book, p. 20.

student wrestling with the basic problem of the authority of the Bible, but it is only through a long drawn out process of nurture, guided at every point by the adult faith of the leaders, that Christian faith will begin to mature. Biblical Christianity will be strengthened if we have the patience to work slowly and soundly along these lines.

CHAPTER TWELVE

THE END

ESCHATOLOGY is one of the great words in Christian thinking. It means simply the doctrine of "last things," such as death, judgment, heaven and hell, and the second coming of Christ (or final judgment day). It is "the end" as far as time is concerned. The problems suggested by eschatology have been in the forefront of Christian thinking in recent years because of the increase in sudden and violent deaths, of the sense of judgment on men's sins, and of the concern of those bereaved with the problem of immortality; and the atom bomb with the suggested possibility of a chain reaction has brought about the old idea of the end of the age or of the world. It has become as relevant to children as to adults in this catastrophic age.

I

Eschatology in the early Church was predominant in the thinking of all the leaders. It appears in Jesus' teachings, in Paul's letters, in the Gospels and Acts, and vividly in Revelation. Salvation, so they believed, would come by a mighty act of God bringing an end to the age. It would be a gracious act of God toward his people, the community of believers, and would bring judgment on all others. The idea of the "new Jerusalem" indicated that a Christian's citizenship was in heaven, and the dead would be raised incorruptible. It was a spiritual concept, for "flesh and blood cannot inherit the kingdom of God." Furthermore, for these early Christians, there was the belief that they were already living in a new age, which existed side by side with the age which God would destroy. When this event did not occur, two possible solutions to the problem were suggested: Revelation placed salvation in the future, while the Johannine material placed the second coming in the advent of the Spirit upon the Church. Both of these views provided an exaggeration of the truth which Jesus taught, that the kingdom is both coming and here.

Immortality was taken for granted in Jesus' teachings, and was interpreted within the eschatological framework we have just mentioned. The only immortality in the New Testament is *resurrection*, and this depends upon repentance and faith. The early Christian experience recorded in the Fourth Gospel includes many passages of significance: "I came that they might have life and have it abundantly. . . . I am the Way, the Truth, and the Life. . . . I am the resurrection and the life. . . . He that believeth on the Son hath eternal life." While there is little specific teaching about immortality in the Gospels, the basic factor in the interpretation of the early Church was Jesus' own resurrection. The conviction that Jesus was still alive was what converted the disciples, convinced them that Jesus was the Messiah, and gave them hope of eternal life. In the earliest teaching it led them also to expect the return of Christ and the institution of the kingdom, but as time went on and this expectation was not fulfilled it was interpreted in terms of personal death and resurrection.

Death is accepted as physically real, and just as Jesus was fully dead, so all men die. While there is no physical resurrection for mankind, it is only by an act of God that men enter the heavenly kingdom. The conditions are moral and spiritual, and "we know that we have passed out of death into life, because we love the brethren." If we fulfill the conditions, we have eternal life now. "Now are we sons of God, and it doth not yet appear what we shall be."

There are some particulars in the New Testament, but the geography and the chronology may safely be ignored. On the whole, Jesus and Paul are reticent about the life beyond the grave, although they always take it for granted. They are more concerned about living in God's way now.

The doctrine of last things, or eschatology, for today, involves our interpretation of death itself, our belief in judgment, and our concern for resurrection.

The finality of death is seen properly against the background of a God of love. "God is love, and he who abides in love abides in God, and God abides in him." Love, to be worth anything, must be dependable. God's working is according to natural law; he has given us a dependable, consistent, and good universe, in which men may by his grace do that which he commands.

This kind of a universe is possible only if man will take the consequences. A series of events, started by some natural cause, may lead to the most tragic experiences. A child dies because of undiagnosed illness; a promising young man is shot down; a wife is killed in an automobile accident. This is not because God willed this particular event, but because God is dependable in his goodness and he will not reverse his laws to help us escape suffering and death.

On the other side of the ledger, death for the very old or the incurable sufferers is a blessing because life has become unendurable. Life without death would be worse than death cutting out life. If the old did not die, we should have to stop the birth of children, and we should have an old folks' hell on earth.

From man's point of view, death is not only inevitable but

desirable. It is the time of death which makes the difference. It seems to be a matter of chance, although chance is an unfortunate word and fate is worse as a description of this interpretation. In our dependable universe, created by a loving God, there are unpredictable happenings. From the perspective of natural law, *after* they have occurred, they are events due to specific causes, but from the point of view of the person who did not will it, it seems to be sheer chance. A good God could not have willed it directly and remained good, yet within God's providence this is the kind of thing that happens every day. It remains a mystery, the kind of mystery which Job had to face when he lost everything and still trusted in Yahweh, for Job had to discover that Yahweh was not like Job. So also the second Isaiah interpreted the meaning of suffering, and saw the difference between man and God.

> " 'For my thoughts are not your thoughts,
>   Nor are your ways my ways,' is the oracle of the Lord,
>   'But as the heavens are higher than the earth,
>   So are my ways higher than your ways,
>   And my thoughts than your thoughts' " (Is. 55:8–9,G).

God's power is not the power of dictatorship; it is the power of love which does not crush personality but which works for man's redemption and salvation. The power of God has always been the power of the Cross, and when one knows that God's power is established through the love and death of Christ, he can bear any kind of evil.

The Cross is God's power, telling us that God has the infinite capacity to endure any evil that man can do or suffer. He does not directly will man's suffering and sudden death, but he suffers from it just as he suffered when the Christ was crucified. How can he bear it all? That is part of the mystery of God; but we know he can, because he did.

It is faith in this kind of love in God that makes the tragedies of life bearable. It does not eliminate or lighten the nature of the tragedy, and the realism of Christianity in saying that death is real and pain is real and sin is real makes for maturity in the rising above tragedy which God's grace makes possible. "There is no fear in love, but perfect love casts out fear" (I Jn. 4:18,A). This maturity is never completely achieved, because man cannot maintain perfect love; but in so far as man loves God because he first loved man, he is freed from fear. The certainty of God's love is the basis for the lack of fear about loved ones who are dead, for they are alive in Christ. "This is the testimony, that God gave us eternal life, and this life is in his Son. He who has the Son has life" (I Jn 5:11–12a,A).

Where a son was killed during the war, the minister gave solace by saying, "It is God's will." The mother accepted this interpretation, but found that her sense of the love of God had vanished, and symptoms of instability began to appear. When a new clergyman called on her, and she said that it was God's will that her son had been taken, he replied, "It wasn't God's will." With clearing eyes, she looked at him and said, "Thank God, you've said that. I couldn't love a God who took my son, but I can love one who permitted men in the horror of war to kill him."

It is not always easy to get the bereaved to Church. There is so much in the corporate worship which provides solace and blessing, that healing should take place. But worship often opens the old wound, and grief is spontaneously greater. It might be likened to the healing of a spinal cyst, where the surgeon's technique is to allow it to heal from the inside out. Every week, there is the painful treatment of the wound with antiseptic washing, and slowly the wound fills in until it is completely healed. It is a rough technique, and needs much pastoral insight when we apply it to the cure of souls.

When all else fails, when defeat has to be faced, when tragedy is irrevocable, when death is final, there are the words of the psalmist:

> "I will lift up mine eyes unto the hills; from whence cometh my help?
> My help cometh even from the Lord, who hath made heaven and earth.
> He will not suffer thy foot to be moved; and he that keepeth thee will not sleep.
> Behold, he that keepeth Israel shall neither slumber nor sleep.
> The Lord himself is thy keeper; the Lord is thy defence upon thy right hand;
> So that the sun shall not burn thee by day, neither the moon by night.
> The Lord shall preserve thee from all evil; yea, it is even he that shall keep thy soul.
> The Lord shall preserve thy going out, and thy coming in, from this time forth for evermore" (Psalm 121,PB).

Poets and theologians have written at length on the nature of life after death. Christian theology insists that there is an after life and that there is judgment, but there is division of opinion concerning most details. Some believe that only this life is a probation, and that judgment comes immediately following death; others advocate either some kind of intermediate state or various levels of heaven; all agree that life after death involves self-consciousness, and very few have taught a "sleep of the soul" until a general resurrection; the fear of hell is still generally held; only great saints go directly to heaven; there will be a final judgment; the final state of the lost is banishment from God, or even oblivion, but may also be unending punishment; there is vagueness about the present state of the saved.[1] Perhaps the best summary, whether we believe in prayers for the dead or not, is found in this phrase: "And we also bless thy holy Name for all thy servants departed this life in thy faith and fear; beseeching thee to grant them continual growth in thy love and service, and to give us grace so to follow their good examples, that with them we may be partakers of thy heavenly kingdom." [2]

It is the nature of God rather than the physiology of man that determines one's belief in immortality. If God places a value on man, then God will give man life everlasting; but man cannot get it on his own account. There is no proof of life beyond the grave, in spite of our belief in the resurrection of Christ; there is only faith. "The Christian hypothesis," says Studdert-Kennedy, "is that life is as good as God revealed in Christ, and that behind the Cross there is ever and always the Resurrection. And it is only by taking this hypothesis, and living life as though it were true, flinging ourselves upon it recklessly in the faith that God keeps the good wine until the last, that we can come to that triumphant certainty which destroys death, and makes us sure that in the midst of death we are in the Life Everlasting." [3]

We are so concerned with the temporal that we assign a time-span to heaven, and yet we know that God who created time is beyond time. When we think of eternal life in terms of timelessness, our whole perspective is changed, for now eternal life is thought of in terms of quality rather than quantity. The experience of eternal life comes now, as the Fourth Gospel makes clear, and yet as long as we are in the temporal order eternal life is in the future. There is nothing automatic about this, and Christianity has never said that all men would

[1] See Frederick C. Grant, *Can We Still Believe in Immortality?* Chicago: Wilcox & Follett, pp. 56–66.
[2] *Book of Common Prayer*, pp. 74–75.
[3] *The Best of Studdert-Kennedy*. New York: Harpers, p. 66.

be saved. The problem is not metaphysical but moral, and men
are not immortal until God makes them so.

The moral issues of life after death are brought out clearly
in a statement by Studdert-Kennedy: "You cannot make a
man fear Hell really until you have made him love God." [4]
The idea of divine judgment finds its origin in prophetic religion, and the idea of the Day of Yahweh was in terms of a
moral evaluation of a people. It is only as people are led to the
vision of God that they have either the hope of eternal life or
the fear of hell, and usually the two emotions are mixed because all men are sinners who wish they were better men. It is
this same moral urgency which runs through the New Testament expectation of the end of the age, when men must repent
now for the kingdom is already at hand. There is a correlation,
therefore, between two ideas: eternal life begins now, there is
a final judgment before God for individuals and for history
itself. The essential meaning of Hell, whether here or here-
after, is exclusion from fellowship with God, and the essential
meaning of Heaven is the experience of that fellowship.

While there is great truth in all the picturesque versions of
death, hell, heaven, and judgment, they may be taken as symbolic of fundamental meanings which cannot be expressed in
prose. We simply do not know what happens or how it happens. There is no empirical evidence that it does occur. Our
thinking begins with the nature of God and the value which
God has placed on man. If God cares enough for man to have
provided for man's redemption, it must be redemption for a
purpose, which is eternal life. If God sees the potential worth
of the individual, then immortality is desirable from God's
point of view. "The confident expectation of eternal life in
its future aspect depends, from the Christian point of view,
upon the goodness and love, the power and wisdom of God,
and upon the fact, in so far as it is a fact, that he has already

[4] *Ibid.*, p. 60.

given us the beginnings of a life of eternal value. . . . Ultimately we must rest our hopes upon the gracious love of God." [5]

II

It is no wonder that many children misinterpret death when we observe how they are guided in such circumstances. If a death occurs which in any way involves them, they are kept out of the sharing of its meaning, or they are given misleading answers, or they feel a sense of mystery which makes it a fearful experience.

Evasion of normal and inevitable facts of life, where those facts are in any way relevant to the child's experience, is a mistake. This is especially true when a parent dies and the child is told, "Daddy's gone away," and they keep repeating the question, "When is Daddy coming back?" Sooner or later the real fact of death must be faced, and children need careful preparation and guidance.

The opposite approach of too much exposure to adult grief may be equally harmful. They should be spared from the hysterical overtones, the morbid feelings, and the wave of sentimentalism which often surround death. Some kinds of funerals are highly emotional and hard on adults and children alike, while others are dignified and express the sense of victory.

Children normally come to the knowledge of death through what happens to their pets, grandparents, and elder friends. Much less frequently is there the death of a parent or a brother or sister. With nursery children and those even younger, it is better that they be protected from observing death. Even in the case of the death of a parent, being present at the funeral or going to the cemetery would not be helpful. The emotional

[5] Douglas Clyde Macintosh, in *Liberal Theology*, ed. by David E. Roberts and Henry Pitney Van Dusen. New York: Scribners, p. 252.

upheaval will still be considerable if it means a change in the child's sense of security, but explanations will not help. The task is to rebuild the sense of belonging and to guard against overprotectiveness by those who do the rebuilding. Normal routine is better than any change.

A four year old girl's mother died in childbirth, and the expected child was also lost. The girl was asleep when her Daddy came home, and nothing was said until twenty-four hours later when she asked:

"Daddy, when will you bring the baby home?"

"There isn't going to be any baby, darling," Daddy replied.

"Why not?"

"Because the baby died."

And then, quick as a flash, "What about Mommy?"

"Mommy died, too."

She burst into tears, crying, "I want my Mommy. I want my Mommy."

There were some explanations and consolations, and she slept fitfully. The next day, she told her playmates that Mommy and Linda had gone to heaven. She stayed with friends during the funeral. After dinner with friends and going home with Daddy, she asked, "Will the baby grow in heaven?"

"Yes, dear," he replied after a prayerful moment, "but not as we do on earth. We have new bodies in heaven."

"Oh, yes," she replied in a very matter-of-fact manner, "you put their bodies in the ground, didn't you?" Nothing had been said to her about the funeral, and Daddy was grateful now that he and Mommy had always tried to answer their daughter's questions simply but as honestly as possible. Once, while driving past the cemetery, her questions had been given simple but honest answers. She wanted to see the grave, and was taken there several days later. "I do not see Mommy," she said, "and I do not see how she can see me with all that dirt on top of her."

"Of course Mommy is not there," said Daddy. "Remember how you said the other day that it is just the body she left behind that is placed in the ground."

"Mommy has a new body now," and she added surprisingly, "Mommy is a spirit now. Mommy is like God." It was this conclusion that made life bearable when she and Daddy had to be separated. At one time she thought Daddy could visit with Mommy in heaven when he took his plane trips to see her.

She decided that Mommy could be with them as God was with them. She talked freely about her Mother, often to the discomfiture of adults. When her playmates taunted her with, "Your Mommy is not here and cannot help you," she would reply, "Yes, she is here, and she does help me."

In the time since her Mother's death, she has learned much from her time of prayer with her Daddy. Because her Mother is included in her prayers and she has had adequate guidance from her Father, she has found other sources of strength and forgiveness often beyond the scope of the average four year old.

Primary children are aware of the fact of death, and will ask questions, such as "Where is heaven?" "Why do they put dead bodies in the ground?" "Why did they burn his body instead of burying it?" They will see and ask about funeral processions. They will need sympathy when a pet dies, for a child's parental instincts are given a more severe jolt by the death of a pet than by the death of a playmate.

Four little girls, aged two, four, six, and eight, knew their mother was seriously ill. Death occurred at night in a hospital and the news was phoned home. The eight year old was still awake and heard the commotion. She was told simply, "Mommy's gone," and then she broke into tears. The next morning the other girls were told, and they listened and understood, but there was no outward emotion. During the day, the four and six year old girls sought out their father and grandmother and asked questions, which were answered calmly. The three older girls were allowed to help their father select their mother's grave, but they did not go to the funeral parlor. The children were kept at home by quarantine and took part in all the activities of the house. They were encouraged to talk freely about their mother. Aunts, uncles, and grandparents, whom they knew well, were helping out. The three older girls went to the funeral, which was held in the church. They joined in the hymns and prayers and whispered a few questions. After the service, a close friend took the girls home while the rest of the family went to the cemetery for the committal. When the family and a few friends arrived home, the girls served them cookies along with coffee. Through it all, the girls showed no emotional upset; and the next day they returned to school. The only symptom of grief was a slight tendency to excitement in the eight year old. All four girls knew what had happened, and they explained it by saying, "Mommy's body is dead, but her spirit is with God." They were quite confident that God would take care of her. The two year old was the most upset emotionally, as she had not seen her mother leave the house to go to the hospital. The emotional continuity was provided by an intelligent and loving grandmother and a father who knew no bitterness in the midst of sheer tragedy.

Juniors will know a great deal about death, not only as experienced but through their reading of newspapers and looking at picture magazines. They will be aware of the danger of accidental death, will see wrecked cars on the highways and pictures of crashed planes in motion pictures, and they will hear of deaths from various kinds of illness. They will know about medicine, and the fight of medical science against disease, especially the highly publicized campaigns against cancer and poliomyelitis. If personal experience has not forced ideas of an after life upon him, this is the best time for study of the Christian idea of eternal life. Careful teaching is necessary to avoid both temporal and geographical blunders, for the junior is beginning to envisage a scientific universe. Three procedures are possible here. When boys and girls are in the sixth or seventh grade, there may be an opportunity for them to attend the funeral of an older person whom they know but whose death is after the promised "three score and ten" years. If it is a dignified funeral in their own Church, with the right kind of hymns and flowers, and preferably with a pall over the casket to symbolize that rich and poor are equal in death under the majestic color of purple, they will begin to see that "death is swallowed up in victory." It has been suggested that the great opening lines of the Prayer Book service will impress the boys and girls and that they will repeat them afterwards: "I am the resurrection and the life, saith the Lord: he that believeth in me, though he were dead, yet shall he live: and whosoever liveth and believeth in me, shall never die" (John 11:25–26).[6]

A second approach, which is effective with both juniors and intermediates, is found in the worship of the Church at Easter. The new life of spring, the great Easter hymns, the story of the resurrection, when seen against the background of the stark realism of the crucifixion, will give a spiritual meaning to death by pointing beyond it. This will be particularly effective if it is backed up by two kinds of study, although a thorough-going approach might have to be postponed to the high school age. The first study would be of the whole story of the passion, from Palm Sunday through Easter, emphasizing the fact that just as Christ was a living Christ for the disciples, so he can be the living Christ for us. The second study might well be based on selections from Paul's great treatment of death and resurrection in his first letter to the Corinthians: "But now is Christ risen from the dead, and become the firstfruits of them that

[6] *Book of Common Prayer*, p. 324; cf. Dora Chaplin, *Children and Religion*, p. 73.

slept. For since by man came death, by man came also the resurrection of the dead" (I Cor. 15:20–21,KJ). "But perhaps someone will ask, 'How is the resurrection achieved? With what sort of body do the dead arrive?' Now that is talking without using your minds! In your own experience you know that a seed does not germinate without 'dying' itself. When you sow a seed you do not sow the 'body' that will eventually be produced, but bare grain, of wheat, for example, or one of the other seeds. God gives the seed a 'body' according to His laws—a different 'body' to each kind of seed. . . . There are illustrations here of the raising of the dead. The body is 'sown' in dishonour; it is raised in splendour. It is sown in weakness; it is raised in power. It is sown a natural body; it is raised a spiritual body. As there is a natural body, so will there be a spiritual body. . . . Just as we have been made like the material pattern, so we shall be made like the Heavenly Pattern. For I assure you, my brothers, it is utterly impossible for flesh and blood to possess the Kingdom of God. The transitory could never possess the Everlasting. . . . This perishable nature of ours must be wrapped in imperishability, these bodies which are mortal must be wrapped in immortality. So when the perishable is lost in the imperishable, the mortal lost in the immortal, this saying will come true:

Death is swallowed up in Victory.

. . . And so, brothers of mine, stand firm! Let nothing move you as you busy yourselves in the Lord's work. Be sure that nothing you do for Him is ever lost or wasted" (I Cor. 15:35–38, 42–44, 49–50, 53–54, 58).[7]

A third approach, which is possible with all ages from the fourth grade and up, depends upon the opportunity offered by

---

[7] J. B. Phillips, *Letters to Young Churches: A translation of the New Testament Epistles*, pp. 64–66. Copyright 1947 by The Macmillan Company (New York) and used with their permission.

death in the congregation or neighborhood. Boys and girls are sensitive to the sorrow of others, and there will be times when the transparency of youngsters offering help to a bereaved family may assist the family in regaining its equilibrium and at the same time provide a lesson in the Christian interpretaton of death and resurrection.

In all these approaches to death and eternal life, there is the harm done by wrong answers. God "took" someone because "God wanted him more than we do." "God helped that alcoholic fall under that truck." "Mother was put in the ground and she can't breathe any more." Johnny died and went to hell because he wasn't baptized."

The problem of evil comes up here in magnified form. "Why did God let Mommy die?" For adults the answer is a mystery. A medical answer will help at some levels, but then there is the question, "Why does God allow bad germs?" It is hard for a child to believe that God can do anything and won't do what he wants. The maturity of Job is hard enough for Jewish and Christian adults. If the faith and trust of children in a loving God is of the Pollyana kind, this attitude will be destroyed by death. Ultimately, it is the kind of God children believe in which will govern their reaction to death. As always, theology is relevant to the experiences of life. It is an empirical fact that God in his wisdom allows death, which we know to be good, and that he also permits premature and undeserved death which from man's point of view is sheer tragedy. Theology must be governed by what God does rather than by what he can do, and this means that while death is a real and final end, it is not the end. The end and destiny of man is to be in eternal fellowship with God.

In olden days, children and adults alike sat through sermons containing vivid descriptions of the fires of hell and rather pale pictures of the glories of heaven. The fear of hell was substituted for the valid "fear" or reverance before God. This is not gone from our midst, although it is uncommon in modern preaching. There are still parents who believe their unbaptized babies are in hell, and often nurses are trained to guard against such oversight. Special burial services are provided for the "heathen" which read like an excuse before God for someone released from Sing Sing Prison.

The idea of judgment is valid. It is essentially a faith in an absolutely moral deity. This judgment works itself out in the experiences of individuals and nations. Children come up against it as soon as they experience the unwielding nature of moral law. It does not need to be put off to a judgment at the time of death, but can be seen operating as men and nations make their own beds in sheol or heaven in this world. With older children there will be plenty of opportunity to discuss the meaning of Hell and Heaven as God's judgment upon the individual after death, and our ignorance is so great that we should be satisfied with saying that Hell is exclusion from fellowship with God, while Heaven is that fellowship fully realized.

Of the idea of a final judgment, there is little that we can teach except with young people in high school or college. This is both a historical and a supra-historical concept, for the final judgment is "beyond history." It points to the fact that historical processes do not exhaust the meaning of God or his creation, and that this world is only a province of God's Kingdom. Earthly life is more than a probationary period or a proving ground, for we can enter eternal life now, but God stands at the end of history as the Judge, and only as man faces God in history and beyond history does the full meaning of man's existence become manifest.

Thus eschatology, or the doctrine of last things, makes the full cycle, and it means that in the end God is sovereign. At death, at the end of an age, at the end of history, there is still God. God minus world equals God, as Archibishop Temple wrote, while world minus God equals nothing. And "nothing" is the perfect description of man without God, while man with God is eternal life.

EPILOGUE

THEOLOGY is relevant to Christian education at every age-level because theology is "truth-about-God-in-relation-to-man." We have taken only a few great theological concepts and illustrated what they mean in this twentieth century on the level of adult thinking and experience and then have translated these great themes in terms of the experiences and capacities of children. We have dealt separately with these guiding ideas, and yet they are valid only when held together in a comprehensive unity. It is such unity of faith that the creeds symbolize, and therefore the creeds are important for the balance that they provide, and in the creeds is always seen clearly the focal point of the Christian Gospel: "God so loved the world that he gave his only begotten Son, that whosoever believeth on him should not perish but have everlasting life."

In this faith we are obedient servants, seeking always God's kingdom and his righteousness, and by the gift of God's grace, we come into his kingdom. The means of grace, which are the gifts of the Holy Spirit, are found in the Church, whose members have a vocation to

"Know thy Son Christ, and seek to make him known." [1]

The Christian grows to maturity within the fellowship and worship of the Church, and in the life and work of the Church God's kingdom is set forward. In spite of the weaknesses of

[1] Edith Clayton, *The Hymnal*, 1940, No. 509.

201

the Church and the sinfulness of its members, the Christian Church is the hope of the world.

Because the Christian religion is the faith of maturity, it is not always easy to nurture that faith among children. Yet there is the teaching of the Master: "Suffer the little children to come unto me, and forbid them not; for of such is the kingdom of God. Verily I say unto you, Whosoever shall not receive the kingdom of God as a little child, he shall not enter therein. And he took them up in his arms, put his hands upon them, and blessed them" (Mk 10:14–16,KJ). This is the challenge facing the Church, and if children can enter the kingdom more easily than adults there must be something more to Christianity than the complexities of theology. Salvation turns on faith and grace, and these are the capacities of which children are the recipients. They have the attitude of trust, and the graciousness to receive all that a loving Father will give them. It is only in such transparent faith that the mature will find salvation.

The other side is this. Paul wrote, "When I was a child, I spoke like a child, I thought like a child, I reasoned like a child; when I became a man, I gave up childish ways" (I Cor. 13:11,A). We need to remember that a child speaks, thinks, and reasons in a childish way, and thus our theology must be relevant to his speaking and thinking, helping him to grow to the level where he can put away childish ways. But we must never destroy his childlike faith, and if we are truly wise we will want that kind of faith for ourselves. We must not be childish before our heavenly Father, but we must be childlike in our faith in him in whom we live and move and have our being.

A BRIEF LIST
OF
RECOMMENDED BOOKS

I. THEOLOGY AND CHRISTIAN EDUCATION

YOUR CHILD'S RELIGION, by Mildred M. and Frank Eakin
(Macmillan, 1942)
>Excellent for its insights into how much theology children of various ages find relevant. Much good common sense, backed by a liberal theology.

CHILDREN AND RELIGION, by Dora P. Chaplin (Scribners, 1948)
>Good Anglican theology applied to real children in a Church school. Also illustrates importance of parents to Christian education.

FAITH AND NURTURE, by H. Shelton Smith (Scribners, 1941)
>A scathing critique of modern Christian education from a conservative theological viewpoint, which did much to inspire this book.

CAN RELIGIOUS EDUCATION BE CHRISTIAN? by Harrison S. Elliott (Macmillan, 1940)
>A theological approach to Christian education which is a criticism of neo-orthodoxy. The books by Smith and Elliott express the opposing tendencies.

THE CHURCH AND CHRISTIAN EDUCATION, by Paul H. Vieth (Bethany Press, 1947)
>Results of recent studies by eminent educators on the importance of theology. The beginning of a movement toward the position expressed in THE CLUE TO CHRISTIAN EDUCATION.

II. PARENTS AND CHRISTIAN EDUCATION

THE MODERN PARENT AND THE TEACHING CHURCH, by Wesner Fallaw (Macmillan, 1947)

One of the best books illustrating the significance of parents in the Church's educational system.

A GREATER GENERATION, by Ernest M. Ligon (Macmillan, 1948)

The story of the greatest parent cooperation achieved by any Christian educational system. This is a basic book for all parents and Church school leaders.

THEIR FUTURE IS NOW, by Ernest M. Ligon (Macmillan, 1939)

An earlier book by Dr. Ligon which gives more information on his unique approach.

CHRISTIAN NURTURE, by Horace Bushnell (Yale University Press, 1947)

A re-issue of the classic expression of the family's role in the Christian nurture of children.

III. THEORY AND PRACTICE OF CHRISTIAN EDUCATION

A GUIDE FOR CHURCH SCHOOL TEACHERS, by Randolph C. Miller (Wilcox & Follett, 1947)

An elementary approach to the theory, method, and theology of Christian education.

THE USE OF THE BIBLE WITH CHILDREN, by Ethel Smither (Methodist Book Concern, 1943)

Shows how the Bible should be used with children of various ages. Indispensable for any course with Bible content.

RELIGION AND THE GROWING MIND, by Basil Yeaxlee (Nisbet, 1939)

One of the best books of all. Being imported regularly.

INDEX

(The page references in bold-face type are the more important references)